GOOD
SHOT

GOOD SHOT

A Guide to Using Clay Target Skills in the Field

STEVEN J. MULAK

Illustrations by the author

STACKPOLE
BOOKS

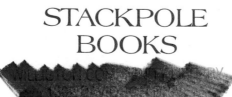

Published by
STACKPOLE BOOKS
5067 Ritter Road
Mechanicsburg, PA 17055
www.stackpolebooks.com

Printed in the United States of America

First edition

10 9 8 7 6 5 4 3 2 1

Cover design by Wendy A. Reynolds
Cover art by Steven J. Mulak
Cover photography by Julia C. Johnson, M & J Outdoor Communication

Library of Congress Cataloging-in-Publication Data
Mulak, Steven J.
    Good shot: a guide to using clay target skills in the field / Steven J. Mulak.—1st ed.
        p. cm.
    ISBN-13: 978-0-8117-0377-2
    ISBN-10: 0-8117-0377-0
    1. Skeet shooting. 2. Trapshooting. I. Title.

GV1181.3.M85 2008
799.3'132—dc22

2007046776

To my dad,
Henry P. Mulak (1919–2007).
His enduring belief in his children proved to be
his greatest gift to them.

CONTENTS

INTRODUCTION

What Is a "Good Shot"?

"That fella's a good shot." I've made that statement about other shooters, and probably, so have you. It's a term of respect based on one essential qualification: the person in question shoots a shotgun well enough to have that excellence recognized by his peers. But just what does it take to be considered a good shot? What do hunters and target shooters mean when they refer to a colleague by that term?

According to Bob Smith of Wilbraham, Massachusetts, a friend whose opinion I value, the definition of a *good shot* amounts to just one word—*consistency*. For him, a good shot is a shooter who routinely finishes with a respectable score, round after round, year after year. Bob knows a lot of shooters who shoot well, but only a few good shots. For Peter Piemonte, another friend who routinely outshoots me at clays, his definition includes the idea that a good shot doesn't miss the same shot twice. That is, a shooter needs to be enough of a scientist to know why he missed the shot and how to go about correcting it.

Of course, both my shooting friends had sporting clays in mind when they offered their definitions. For field shooting, I've long agreed with my dad's broad interpretation: a good shot doesn't miss the easy ones. Let the difficult shots fall where they may, but when you've got an easy shot, make sure you don't miss. Not ever. If that's you, in my Dad's book you'd be a good shot. And I'd agree with him: missing easy shots ought to disqualify you from even being considered.

But recently I've begun to think there's more to it than that. My own latest take on the definition of a *good shot* is someone who is genuinely surprised when the bird doesn't fold dead in the air. The insinuation, of course, is that the good shot passes on chancy opportunities and low-percentage shots, but when the time comes to shoulder the gun, the good shot does so with confidence that the shot can be made. It's not that a good shot doesn't miss; it's that he or she truly expects to make a clean kill after deciding that the shot is a "go."

Of course, that leads to the question, "Why even bother?" Sports involving gunpowder are widely suspect in this day and age. Yesteryear's rugged frontiersmen might be a source of pride for the average American. Note the Currier and Ives prints featuring bird dogs and hanging game and hunters in action decorating many inns and restaurants, along with decoys, hunting horns, and the paraphernalia of muzzle-loading weapons—all part of our past culture. Yet today, there are words we don't dare say out loud in civilized society, and *gun* is near the top of that list. If we read society's opinion correctly, it seems that hunting is okay, as long as it was done in the distant past.

We don't know what to do about hunting. We can't seem to make up our minds about how to behave in this deadly game we pursue. There is a body of outdoor literature that tells us we have a right to go hunting, then urges us not to kill anything. Catch-and-release may be an option when using a fishing rod, but not when you go afield with a shotgun. "Kill with principles," we're told. "Hunt, but don't be too successful." In these politically correct times, we don't know how we should perceive what we're doing. And we're constantly attempting to justify it—not so much to others, but to ourselves.

I'm not out to change anyone's mind. But if you're afield with a shotgun, there are reasons to shoot well. Arguments are frequently made that a good shot wastes a lot less game than a poor shot who cripples birds that can't be retrieved. Maybe so. But at the heart of the matter is the idea that if you're going to do something—anything—you ought to do it well. Simply shooting a shotgun doesn't take much skill, but shooting it well certainly does. It doesn't come easy. Anyone who is a good shot didn't arrive there by accident. This book is an attempt to get you there, or at least show you the way.

Separating Truth
from Myth

People who should know better say that shotgunning is an art. Defining what is meant by an *art* can be tricky, but any definition always includes the terms *imagination, creativity,* and *originality.* When you're trying to hit a flying target with a shotgun, you're not so much shooting at something as shooting where something is going to be a moment from now. Admittedly, that takes a little imagination, but does that make it art? Adding to the shotgunning-as-art idea is the fact that a shotgunner doesn't really use gun sights per se—at least not on flying targets. When you're shooting correctly, the barrel and the bead are blurred in your vision, so you're not really aiming at all—you're following a moving object with your eyes while holding a shotgun. You've got to be a little bit creative to do that, but is that art?

Then there's something I call the "invisibility factor" that adds to the air of mysticism. We point the shotgun and pull the trigger, and something happens that we can't see. We see only the effects (or the lack thereof)—the target breaks or it doesn't, the bird is hit or it keeps flying. But the process itself—the shot in flight—is invisible. If you could see what was going on (as in archery or golf), shooting would be considered an athletic undertaking. But the invisibility factor somehow makes it a creative art form—at least in some people's opinion.

In truth, when the shotgunning-as-art argument comes up, someone is usually trying to convince you of something illogical, such as: Shot stringing is beneficial on crossing targets. Or inconsistency is an inescapable part of shotgunning. Or little guns perform as well as big ones. Or a single pellet of such-and-such size is all you need to knock down a gamebird. Or mixed shot sizes work well. Or square shot is good for opening up a pattern. Or more is less (or vice versa). None of this is logical, and none of it is true.

Shotgun shooting is not art. It is an application of the laws of physics with a little athleticism thrown in. To call something an art implies that people who do it well have some God-given talent, while others who don't, don't. That may be true of forms of expression such as music and painting, but it is hardly true of shotgunning. Rather, shotgunning is a learned skill that takes some effort to acquire. Like any applied science—from cooking to golfing to riding a bike—if you do it right, results follow. There is no mysticism involved, no special talent, no secret trick, no art. You just need to practice and pay attention to a few basic things, which are the subject matter of this book.

It's often difficult to separate the facts from the many dubious beliefs that people mindlessly repeat. Supposition, superstition, and the momentum of tradition cloud the science of shotgunning. In that mess of misinformation, you need to find the kernels of truth and hang on to them, because they are essential if you want to become a good shot. Following is a list of a dozen such indispensable verities. Each represents an important concept in good shooting and is elaborated on later in this book.

1. Good shotgunning can be learned. But if good shooting can be learned, so can bad shooting. A lifetime of bad habits can be difficult to unlearn, but improved results predictably follow improved methods. In chapter 3, bad habits and their correction are addressed, as well as some techniques to improve your shooting away from the target range. Remember, you will get better with practice.

2. In shotgunning, there are only two rules of marksmanship: find the flight line of the target, and keep the gun moving. Everything else is an elaboration of these two basic tenets. Finding the flight line and moving the gun along it may be easier said than done, however, particularly when time is short and conditions are less than ideal. But if there is "a trick to it," there it is. The common question of "How much lead?" makes for interesting discussions, but there is really only one answer: *find the line and keep the gun moving.* If you can arrive at a comprehensive understanding of these two points and

Good shotgunning can be learned.

apply that understanding to your shooting, you can throw away every book ever written on shotgunning (including this one).

3. Every miss should automatically translate into a lesson. Hitting all the targets is never a realistic goal, but knowing what you did wrong when you miss certainly is. Practice is all about getting in tune with your shooting abilities so that you can learn something positive from a missed shot and, hopefully, correct it. Skeet shooting is a good place to start and a logical departure point (see chapter 2).

4. Gamebirds are easy to hit but difficult to kill. Simply knocking down a gamebird is not enough—a clean kill is what you're after. There are two theories regarding the best way to accomplish that end: the penetration method versus the shock-effect method. In chapter 5, I argue that shock is a consistent killer of gamebirds, while physical trauma is not.

5. Successful shotgunning in the field involves a lot more than marksmanship. Hunting involves gun handling, outdoor skills, and an understanding of the habits of the gamebird you're after—plus an intelligent application of those factors over a prolonged period. It all comes under the heading of wing shooting, which is covered in chapters 7 and 8.

6. There is one right gauge, choke, and load combination for every shooting situation. The argument goes that if one load or choke is better than another for your specific hunting situation, there must be one best combination. Find it, and consistency follows (see chapter 5).

7. Pattern quality trumps every other consideration in shotgun performance. Your intention is never to hit a bird with all the pellets that come out of the end of the barrel—but you do want to hit it with some of them. The quality of the pattern ensures that "some" is a sufficient and constant quantity. Good patterns are responsible for predictable performance, and they are far more important than muzzle velocity, shot size, or load volume (see chapter 5).

8. Pattern density is the first limit on the range of a shotgun. In all things related to shotgunning, the measure of effectiveness is consistency. Good shooting—that is, producing consistent, predictable results—involves an awareness of both range and pattern. Chapter 5 addresses the need to establish an effective "slot" for your field shooting—one where you're sure of a consistently effective pattern through the full length of a 10-yard swath.

9. Most problems with shotgunning can be traced to the invisibility factor. That phenomenon leads to numerous bad decisions. When shooters start to believe things that border on the superstitious, it is almost always a function of the invisibility factor. Investigation, however, can provide an understanding of those things that can't be readily seen. Without such investigation, we operate far more on hope than faith. In chapter 5, you'll learn what you can do to overcome the invisibility factor and reach the point of knowing what your shotgun can and—almost as importantly—cannot do.

10. You can be a good shooter in spite of an inferior shotgun, but it's not easy. The list of prerequisites for an effective field gun is brief. The foremost consideration is that there is a difference between a cleanly killed gamebird and a chipped clay target. Opinions on firepower and handling characteristics vary when the subject is the "right" gun. Chapter 4 attempts to separate the gladiators from the gladioli.

11. Modern premium ammunition is better than anything made in the past. That fact alone makes many of the definitions and opinions of the past obsolete, yet they persist. As a result of these erroneous beliefs, the typical American shotgunner is using one choke too tight and one shot size too coarse (see chapter 6).

12. "You better like the outdoors, because there's not enough hunt in hunting to go afield for hunting alone." That's a quote from my father, and in this age of short seasons, limited bags, and a scarcity of game, his words were never truer. Here, at the beginning of the twenty-first century, being an outdoorsman and being a hunter are not necessarily the same, but it is becoming increasingly difficult to pursue the latter for a few months of the year without also making a full-time avocation of the former. The two wing-shooting chapters elaborate on this premise.

If I were to add a 13th truth, it would be this: you *can* become a good shot. There is no doubt in my mind, even though I've never seen you shoot. If you believe it, too, then we've made a start.

Skeet Revisited

"Skeet shooting and bird hunting are about as similar as paging through a *Playboy* magazine is to taking out a cute divorcee for dinner and cocktails." I wrote that observation for a shooting article, and I still think it's pretty funny—and true. In the case of the *Playboy* magazine, it's all about make-believe. You can take your time; there's no hurry. You can even turn the pages backward if you missed something or want a better look. But the dinner and cocktails is real: you need to react to a changing situation whether you're ready or not. You can't go back and start over if you make a mistake. There are no guarantees.

Similarly, everything in skeet shooting is predictable. Nothing happens until you call for the target. You know in advance where it's going, and unless you're in a contest of some sort, you can always "turn the pages backward" by calling for the target again if you'd like another chance. In contrast, in the field, you're on your own. Sometimes a pointing dog can add a modicum of predictability by showing you in advance where the bird might be, but you still need to react to a changing situation and do it right now. You can't go back and start over if you make a mistake, and there are no guarantees.

Skeet was invented sometime around 1925 by a group of Massachusetts bird hunters. Among them was William Harnden Foster, author of the classic *New England Grouse Shooting.* The game started out as a form of grouse-shooting practice, but smashing flying targets with a shotgun turned out to be so much fun that it quickly became popular among people who had never even seen a grouse, let alone hunted one. Competition, as it does in all things, fueled a rapid evolution of game-specific shooting methods, and skeet became 20 precise and repetitive movements that were hardly recognizable as those practiced by grouse hunters. With popularity came commercialism, and soon there were skeet vests, skeet guns, skeet loads, and skeet shoes. By 1940, even its inventor bemoaned what had become of the game he originated.

Fortunately, the evolution of skeet involved only how the game was played, not the game itself.* We can use skeet shooting to stay in practice for bird shooting because, physically, it's still the same game that Foster and his buddies invented: same targets, same distances, same speed. You don't need a skeet gun or anything special to shoot skeet—you can do it with the same gun you hunt with.

Some things seem obvious, but I'll state them anyway. Skeet is not bird shooting. Real birds accelerate and rise once they leave the ground; clay targets do just the opposite. Birds have a way of taking flight when you least expect it, but in skeet, nothing happens until you say "pull." Birds in flight can and do change direction; clay targets occasionally get wind blown, but essentially they follow a predetermined flight path every time. Gamebirds fly faster and slower, nearer and farther, lower and higher, and rarely as straight as skeet targets do.

Despite these differences, skeet remains the single most important shortcut to figuring out how to hit moving targets, including all manner of gamebirds. The day is gone when a hunter could learn to shoot well just from hits and misses while hunting. Seasons are short, bag limits are small, and gamebirds are hardly plentiful. If you're ever going to become a good shot, you need to become

---

* Originally, the skeet field was a complete circle and the game was called "around the clock." As the game became more popular, consideration had to be given to where the shots were ultimately falling, and out of necessity, the skeet field took on its familiar half-circle configuration. Although I can't think of any skeet setup where it would be safe to do so, it might be instructive to shoot the course from the negative side of the field. You'd see the high-house targets as right-to-lefts and the low-house offerings from a similar reverse angle.

intimate with clay targets, and more so than any of the other clay target games, skeet allows you to work out the problems of shotgun marksmanship.

Complicating all things shotgun is the previously mentioned invisibility factor. When we miss a bird in the field, we often don't know why. We ask ourselves: Did I shoot too soon? Too late? Did I stop the gun? Was I above the bird? If another bird got up in a similar manner a minute later, we'd have a chance to try something different. Unfortunately, that doesn't happen. We might see another shot like that before the season is out, but then again, we might not. In the field, we're usually given a large dollop of time to stew about a missed shot. Sometimes, during that stewing time, bird hunters will arrive at conclusions that are not always correct. Men become desperate and change shells, change chokes, change guns—all because they don't really know why they missed.

There's no such problem at the skeet range. Each shot is predictable and repeatable and offers an opportunity to work on specific problem areas. You can say, "Let me have that one again," and keep trying different solutions until you find the right one. If you're willing to pay for the extra targets, you can shoot the same shot over and over until the trap machine is empty or your shoulder falls off, whichever comes first.

Some shooters truly expect to hit all the targets. For them, every miss is a mistake. That may be a workable theory at the target range, but not in the uplands and waterfowl marshes. In field shooting, never missing is hardly a realistic goal. However, knowing what you did wrong when you miss is something worth striving for. Skeet can provide that knowledge.

The game of skeet offers a universal frame of reference for all shotgun shooters. The various shots are those we see while hunting, and nearly every bird hunter understands what is meant when a shot is referred to as a "high-house two" or a "station eight." Of course, the translation is rarely so direct: usually, it's "high-house two, but lower and curving away," or "station eight, but with the bird climbing steeply."

For a bird hunter on the skeet field, station one high house replicates the situation in which a treed grouse loses its nerve as the

High-one as a pheasant shot.

hunter walks beneath. Similarly, rooster pheasants are known to rise and then level off, offering an underneath-type shot as they fly away. Duck hunters sometimes see the same shot when a bird buzzes over the rig from behind the blind. It takes some practice, because the sight picture required is counterintuitive. The overhead line of the target's flight goes straight away from the hunter. The difficulty is that the bird is flying level to the ground (or nearly so) and presents a weird perspective to the shooter. You must get in front of a moving target to make a hit, but in this case, "in front" is actually underneath.

To hit high-one, swing the gun along the flight path of the target (which, from your perspective, is nearly straight down) and pull the trigger the instant you pass the bird. As with every other situation on the skeet field, when you miss, it's usually a matter of not keeping the gun moving right through the shot—in shooting terms, you "checked." That is, you unconsciously stopped the gun as you pulled the trigger. If you keep the gun moving, the target will break.

Both high-two and low-six are wonderfully quick quartering shots, albeit from opposite directions. They are as fast and true as any hunting situation when the bird flushes on the flank and breaks across in front of you. It's a common shot in the field, and we all need work on these angles. The target line is the classic quartering shot. The left-to-right high-house two starts 8 feet higher and is

Low-six is a classic quartering shot.

flatter than the climbing right-to-left out of the low house. Pull along the flight line of the target, and keep the gun in front of the bird as you fire; then, as with every target, follow through after the shot. The most common reason for missing this one is riding the bird too long and not being able to keep the gun from "rainbowing" off the flight line. The rainbow effect is detailed in chapter 8, but for now, it's enough to know that long swings tend to curve downward. Trying to take this shot once the target has passed well beyond the center stake nearly guarantees that you'll pull the gun off the line of the target. The solution is to find the line—it slopes upward from the low house and (apparently) downward from the high house. Swing the gun, fire quickly, and follow through.

Low-one and high-seven are angled incomers; low-two and high-six are the same, but with more angle. I lump the four together because this type of shot is supposed to represent a bird that was driven in your direction by your partner or perhaps by a flushing dog. When hunting, this is inevitably a fast and memorable opportunity. Unfortunately, on the skeet field, shooters sometimes wait them out and take the target as a floater when it begins to slow and drop. Too bad. For this shot to be good practice, you should take the bird while it's still rising. Taken quickly, these incomers can be challenging shots.

On these four targets the line of the bird is steeply rising, so lift your gun along the flight line, and fire as soon as you pass the incoming target—not much lead is required. The difficulty with this method is that you don't see the target as you pull the trigger—the gun barrel has blotted it out. If you miss, chances are you peeked because you wanted to see the target break. In golf, all you see when you lift your head too soon is a bad shot; here, the outcome is the same, so don't peek. Find the line of the incoming target, and keep the gun moving.

What you get at station eight are two shots that you might see a few times each season in the thick stuff: jackrabbit-quick incomers that you shoot almost in self-defense. Station eight is a trick shot that is all but impossible unless you've seen it dozens of times and worked out the kinks. In the field, of course, you wouldn't take this

High-eight is a trick shot.

Low-seven as a quail shot.

shot—at least, not if you expected to eat the bird. Instead, you'd turn around and take the bird going away. But don't try that on the skeet field—the people standing behind you won't appreciate it.

On station eight the line of the bird is coming right back over your head, or nearly so. At this range, your pattern is only the size of a cantaloupe, so this shot depends on timing. The instructions for how to hit station eight are the same as for the previous four—except that they're written with an exclamation point at the end: lift the gun along the flight line, blot out the incoming target, and fire—but do it quicker! And if there is anything niftier in the game of skeet than centering a station eight target and turning it into a smoke ball, I don't know what it is. If you miss, your timing was off or, more likely, you lifted your head.

Low-seven is supposed to be a layup. It represents the sort of shot you get when the dog points and you walk in and flush the bird. Even if real gamebirds don't always get up immediately in front of you, most field shots are classic rising straightaways of the low-seven type. In the field, gamebirds may hook left or right or get behind a tree, or sometimes they give you that humpbacked up-and-down flight pattern that you can't stay on. Some are less difficult than others, but real birds are never quite as easy as when you're standing on the concrete pad with your back to the house.

You don't need to move the gun much on low-seven, but you do have to lift the muzzle to stay with the bird as it rises—a still muzzle will translate into a miss. This is a good station to begin practicing your gun mount if you're unaccustomed to shooting "low gun." Both in the field and on the skeet range, it's easy to put too much energy into the gun mount and see that extra momentum carry the muzzle higher than you intended. There's more on the subject of gun impetus in chapter 8, but for now, it's enough to know that when low-seven is missed, it's usually a case of unexpected momentum. The best solution is to imagine that you're bayoneting the bird as it flies away—thrust the gun forward, then snap the butt straight back into its mounted position. That keeps the muzzle movement to a minimum.

Stations three, four, and five are what we practice for. They're difficult crossing shots that come naturally to no one. Crossing pheasants or landing ducks might not be going this fast, but bobwhites, grouse, and doves will be. Low-three and high-five are absolute 90-degree shots requiring more lead than anything else on the skeet

High-three is a 45-degree angle crossing shot.

field. Low-five, however, is the most frequently missed target of all, probably because it has so much upward slope to its flight line that it disappears from sight right around the time a right-handed shooter is pulling the trigger.

Crossing shots require a big lead and a smooth swing, complete with an exaggerated follow-through. These targets are almost always missed behind, and it's easy to misinterpret the amount of lead needed. However, once you get the proper sight picture down pat, the most common cause for shooting behind these crossing shots is failure to maintain the swing speed. When you get as far in front as these targets require, you sometimes chicken out and slow the muzzle. Another reason for missing is that you're aiming so far ahead that you want to peek back at the target and lift your head to do so. Make sure that you're well in front of the target, swing smoothly on the line, and keep the gun moving.

A gunshot travels pretty quickly, but it's not instantaneous. It takes about $\frac{1}{12}$ second for a shot to go 23 yards, which is the distance to the center stake on a skeet field. A crossing target (or bird) flying at 30 miles per hour moves 4 feet in that tiny instant of time. Add to the equation the fact that human reaction time averages $\frac{1}{4}$ second. That is, the same target will travel another 11 feet in that built-in lock time between your brain and your trigger finger. So if you shoot right at the crossing target with a dead-still gun, you'll miss it by 15 feet. Yikes. Does that mean that the correct lead on the two right-angle targets (high five and low three) is 15 feet? If you don't move the gun at all, the answer is yes. Of course, nobody practices that sort of shooting. Instead, you're encouraged to shoot while swinging the gun and leading the target.

On the subject of swinging and leading, if you spend any amount of time at the skeet club, you'll invariably hear other shooters talking about leads in terms like "three feet," or "a-foot-and-a-half." For proponents of that school of thought, measured leads are the only way to go. But since I've never seen a yardstick out in the sky 23 yards away, I don't have much faith in that sort of "exact measurement" advice. Looking back over my instructions at the various stations, I haven't said much about leads, other than vague references to "not much lead" or "a big lead." Lead is important—there's no denying it—but the pattern is fully a yard across, so it's conceivable that you can be off by 3 feet and still hit the bird. Nobody misses a target because their foot-and-a-half lead was off by a few inches.

I reiterate: there are only two fundamentals to hitting a moving target—find the line of the bird, and keep the gun moving. Nothing else really matters. When you miss a target on the skeet range, it's because you improperly carried out one or the other. Finding the line requires concentration—you have to look for it. It's a matter of combining observation with imagination. Skeet is good training, because the same line is traced each time the target is thrown, and errors in interpretation are easily identified. Sometimes the line is misread—high two is a glaring example. What you're looking for is the actual flight path of the target, which may be quite different from where you instinctively suppose it will be. Finding the actual line the gun has to move along is the only way to know where the target will be by the time the shot gets there. When targets are missed above or below, it's usually because of a misread flight line.

Keeping the gun moving is difficult, because your body is reluctant to do so. You swing the gun just fine, but somehow, your body interprets pulling the trigger as the conclusion of that swinging motion—a period at the end of a sentence. That's a mistake, both in thought and in deed, because your body unconsciously begins to stop the gun in anticipation of the swing's conclusion. When that happens, the gun movement slows, and you'll miss behind. You may think that you're not slowing the gun, but your body doesn't always do what the brain tells it to. A conscious exaggeration of the follow-through after the shot is the solution to the problem.* That is, keep the muzzle swinging along the flight line of the target for a long time after the trigger is pulled. Since it is physically impossible to stop the gun if you're exaggerating a follow-through, it's a sure cure for the problem.

In reality, the words *solution* and *cure* are not entirely accurate, because they imply a permanent fix. *Antidote* might be a better choice of words. Like nearly every bad habit in shotgunning, the tendency to stop the swing will come creeping back as soon as you let your

---

* My own follow-through mantra is to mentally repeat the declarative "Hit the bird" as I swing the gun. I pull the trigger on the word *the* and don't stop the gun's swing until I've gotten the word *bird* out.

guard down. Better advice is to know that there is an antidote for the problem, and the prescription is to take a heavy dose of that remedy whenever the symptoms reoccur.

Bad habits are not limited to misreading the line and stopping the swing. There is also the sin of "coming out of the gun," in which the shooter is in such a hurry to get the gun off the shoulder that the shot is affected. Another problem is riding the target too long, with the resultant rainbow effect in the swing. Putting unnecessary impetus into the gun mount also works against accuracy. Yet another bad habit is limiting the swing's arc by not moving from the hips. These faults are taken up in the wing-shooting chapters.

Being the predictable game that skeet is, several different schools of thought have evolved on how best to break targets. Some shooters make a big deal of the distinction between moving the gun faster than the target and overtaking it, as opposed to getting the gun in front and matching the speed of the target. No matter which philosophy you follow, if you don't find the line and keep the gun moving, you might as well be rearranging deck chairs on the *Titanic*. I have been watching people miss skeet targets for 40 years, and with very few exceptions, every miss can be attributable to the failure to follow one those two fundamentals.*

It's time to repeat something stated earlier: *skeet is not hunting*. It's a game that's all about marksmanship and nothing else. Even though you might use skeet to practice field techniques, the game provides no reward for having a smooth gun mount, using the safety properly, or reloading quickly. There is no built-in incentive for knowing when to shoot hurriedly and knowing when you can take extra time. Being

---

* Occasionally, a missed target is actually the gun's fault. Tight chokes can result in a too-small pattern at the close ranges seen in skeet—there's not much to be learned from a miss when the 26-yard pattern is the size of a grapefruit. Much less common is the much-ballyhooed point-of-impact problem wherein the gun does not hit where it's aimed. Gun writers like to make a big deal of the idea, but outside of one cheap double imported from Turkey, I've never encountered a gun that didn't hit within inches of the spot where it was pointed. In truth, you might spend a lifetime with a shotgun that impacted off-center by a few inches and never suspect that it wasn't bull's-eye-accurate. We're not shooting dimes with a .22, after all. Serious point-of-impact problems can be disastrous, but they are rare, and all but unknown in good-quality guns.

able to anticipate and react to the unpredictable doesn't come into play in skeet. It's a game that's only about marksmanship.

But if you're a bird hunter looking to improve your marksmanship, welcome to the skeet field. You've come to the right place. If skeet is new to you, you might break 10 or 12 on your first round. Getting to the point where you can regularly break 20 or 22 might take a dozen rounds, if you're paying attention. The how-to knowledge you'll pick up along the way will make you a better wing shot. Skeet gives you as many chances as you need to figure out why you always miss those out-of-the-tree shots, and you'll gain an understanding of the correct sight picture for those fast-crossing birds.

But on the skeet range, there's a difference between *knowing* how to break them all and actually breaking them all. Some people drive themselves crazy in the clay target games because they've achieved the former but can't seem to succeed at the latter. Inevitably, that leads to bad decisions. In their quest for perfection, some people cross the line and become "skeeters." They take the safety off ahead of time (I've even known skeet shooters to have the safety removed from their shotguns), premount the gun, and "groove in" on the target line. They become fussy about what part of the pad they stand on and the direction in which their toes are pointing. They are easily distracted and need absolute quiet as they prepare to shoot. They remove as many variables from the clay target equation as possible, and every step leads them closer to perfection. And it works. Follow their example, and you'll break more targets—if that's your goal. But none of the skeeter's methodology translates into more birds in your bag when you go hunting. In fact, exactly the opposite is true—if you become a skeeter, you won't learn and practice the skills needed to hunt successfully. So ask yourself: Are you a bird hunter who's trying to become a good shot? Or are you a skeet shooter in pursuit of perfection?

If becoming a good shot is not about marksmanship, it's because that part is a given—you can quickly become as good a marksman as you need to be. Skeet is the shortcut: the target will break if you find the line and keep the gun moving. Ignore either of those rules and the result is a miss, both on and off the skeet field. It's not even difficult.

Starting Over, Getting Better, and Taking Your Shooting Afield

Every day, we do things that at one time required some thought, but because we've done them so many times, they now seem to happen automatically: eating with a fork, tying our shoe laces, driving a standard-shift automobile, typing on a keyboard. At one time, we had to learn to do those things, and doing them well required practice. But after a while, we could do those tasks without diverting our attention from other activities that might require our concentration. Some of my intellectual friends refer to the process as moving the task from the declarative memory to the implicit memory—the part of the brain that handles procedural tasks.

Among these automatic responses stored in your brain, some may not necessarily be welcome. For instance, I started out squinting one eye when I shouldered a gun—following the example set in all those cowboy movies I saw as a kid. And it was something I had to unlearn. This chapter covers the things you need to learn—or perhaps unlearn—before you take the next step on the road to becoming a good shot. If you don't believe you have any bad habits or counterproductive methods you need to overcome, answer the following questions to see how well you go about the business of shooting while in the field.

How natural is your gun mount? Getting the gun into position promptly when the time arrives is a tricky business. The motion ought to be fluid and automatic, but it rarely is unless you've done some practicing. This book is about identifying and addressing the differences between target shooting and hunting situations, and here is the first one. A champion skeet shooter who can't bring down one bird during a morning full of pheasant flushes hasn't suddenly become a poor shot. Rather, that shooter has never bothered to figure out how to quickly get gun to shoulder while walking around—resulting in an unending series of botched opportunities in the field.

Once you have a general idea of how to hit a moving target, make mounting the gun an integral part of every shot. You need to put all the elements together, because you'll never become familiar with the dynamics of field shooting unless you rehearse them. Any shooting practice you do should include every step: mounting the gun, working the safety, swinging on the target, and firing. Think of the whole cycle as the complete shot, and do it every time you shoot—not just when you're shooting for keeps. In the field, it should all be second nature to you, which means that you've got to practice every move, start to finish.

At the range, you won't break as many targets as you would with the gun premounted, but breaking targets isn't the point here. In fact, you don't have to actually shoot the gun to rehearse what you need to do. Even at home indoors with an unloaded shotgun, it's amazing how adept you can become just by handling it once in a while. Invest in some snap-caps for dry-fire practice, and keep the gun handy. It'll drive your spouse crazy, but there are worse things you could be doing.

Later, you'll have to consider carrying positions and the inertia that accompanies gun movement as part of the complete-shot equation. But for now, it's enough to understand that gun mounting must become an automatic part of every shot.

Can you move the gun fluidly once it's at your shoulder? There is one correct shotgun-shooting posture: head leaned into the gun, your cheek resting on the comb of the butt stock; left arm supporting the weight of the gun; body bent forward to absorb the recoil

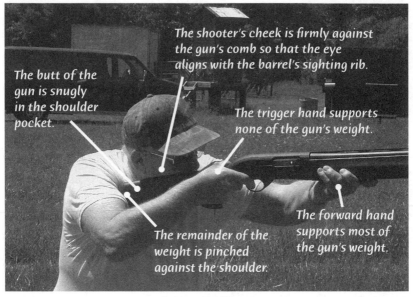

The shooter's cheek is firmly against the gun's comb so that the eye aligns with the barrel's sighting rib.

The butt of the gun is snugly in the shoulder pocket.

The trigger hand supports none of the gun's weight.

The remainder of the weight is pinched against the shoulder.

The forward hand supports most of the gun's weight.

The tangled knot.

properly; shooting hand relaxed on the grip; gun butt firmly in the pocket of your shoulder. That arrangement is, for want of a better term, the "tangled knot" of shoulders, face, hands, arms, and shotgun.

For this posture to be correct, your master eye* must be in the exact location to serve as the shotgun's rear sight—the eye looks along the barrel's rib, and the gun points right where you're looking. Getting into the tangled knot easily is why you practice gun mounting. Staying in it—that is, keeping the knot "tightly tied" while you swing the gun along the line of the target—takes some doing. With so many parts, the knot is easily loosened, and anything more than a slight movement tends to move your face out of sighting alignment.

---

* Just as we are left- or right-handed, we are left- or right-eyed. To determine which is your dominant eye, or "master eye," point at something with both eyes open. While maintaining your point, close first one eye and then the other. You'll find that your pointed finger is right on target with your master eye, but off to the side with the other. In most cases, the master eye agrees with handedness—that is, right-handed people tend to have a right master eye. In shotgunning, when the two don't agree,

The most common way for the knot to become untied is by lifting your head off the stock. It's a well-known and obvious mistake. If you lift your head, the gun's "rear sight" no longer looks where the barrel is pointing, and you'll invariably miss over the top of the target. Why do so many shooters lift their heads? At the start of the mount, you lean naturally into the gun, but the tendency is to straighten up as you turn to the right or left. When the back straightens, the head comes up and off the stock. There are other reasons why shooters lift their heads and miss the target, but we'll get to those later. For now, it's enough to realize that

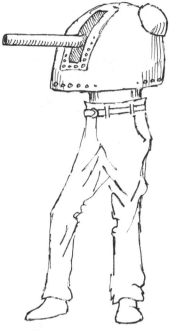

Become a gun turret.

the knot has to remain snugly tied, and the lock-up of face and stock comb is always the first part of the knot to come unraveled.

Moving the gun with just your arms is a less obvious mistake, but equally wrong. It causes the gun to pivot out of alignment with the sighting eye. You've got to be very lucky to hit anything with your cheek off the stock. To prevent such unraveling, move the gun by rotating the hips rather than the arms. I tell beginners to think of themselves as a battleship's gun turret once the gun is mounted. The weirder the shot, the more important it becomes to stay locked up above the waist. To hit below-eye-level crossers, hooking shots, and

---

shooting with both eyes open becomes a problem. This can happen to anyone, but it seems to be especially prevalent in longtime shooters later in life. To get around the problem, they begin to shoot with one eye closed and experience all the disadvantages of monocular vision. The remedy can be as simple as a small transparent but blurry dot affixed in the right spot on the shooter's glasses. When positioned correctly, this prevents the "off eye" from focusing on the target at the time of the shot.

station eight incomers, the eye-barrel alignment must be maintained as you move the gun. Keep the knot tightly tied by swiveling from the hips.

Do your feet move naturally into a good shooting posture? Getting into a shooting position while carrying the gun in the field ought to be as easy as walking. That said, it should be noted that some people have a lot of trouble with footwork, but it's really not that difficult.

You can't shoot straight ahead if you're standing square to the target—at least, you can't shoot very comfortably or very accurately that way. Everyone seems to shoot best by pointing the gun across the body just forward of the "off" shoulder (for right-handed shooters, that would be to the left). You wouldn't need to be concerned with footwork if birds always appeared at "10 o'clock high," where they'd be easy to hit, but of course, they don't. In the field, it becomes necessary to use a bit of footwork to achieve the correct alignment.

The one-step.

If this basic repositioning were a dance, it would be called the "one-step." For right-handers, it involves taking a step with your left foot and letting your hips follow as you mount the gun. Footwork enhances the entire dynamic: the step naturally shifts your weight forward and starts your head leaning properly as you mount the gun. It points your shoulder and the gun's muzzles in the correct direction. The one-step helps everything else happen correctly.*

Stepping with your left foot is basic—it's not the Ali shuffle or anything Fred Astaire might have to teach you. The one-step should be an integral part of the gun mount and the complete shot, but for some reason, it's made out to be much more complicated. There's more on footwork and shooting in chapters 7 and 8, but for now, just practice the one-step when you shoot on the skeet field. Then it won't seem foreign to you when the time comes to shoot while you're walking around.

Do you shoot with one eye closed? Keeping both eyes open is the most elementary of shotgunning's tenets. The main reason to do so is that depth perception is all but impossible with one eye closed. One-eyed sighting might work with rifles and stationary targets, but not when you're using a shotgun and the target is flying by. In addition, focus, field of vision, and low-light sensitivity are greatly improved when both eyes are permitted to work together.

You don't "aim" a shotgun** so much as "follow the gun's point." You have to be focused out where the target is, and for that, you need

---

* Throughout this book, my instructions are tailored to right-handed shooters, at the expense of the 1-in-25 shotgunners who are left-handed. My writing is boring enough without repeating everything a second time, so let me apologize to southpaws everywhere and make the obligatory blanket-statement that "lefties need to reverse the handedness of my instructions." On a similar note, I universally speak of shooters as "men," even though I know of a number of women who hunt birds and handle shotguns very well. I therefore apologize in advance to anyone of female persuasion who might look to my book for instruction and find it too insensitive to gender differences.

** The sight bead on the barrel is a misnomer: it's there to check your alignment when you're *not* shooting. You put the gun to your shoulder to see how the bead and the target line up, and from there, you can determine whether the gun fits. But when you're wing shooting—correctly, that is—the barrel and the sight bead are blurred.

Shoot with both eyes open.

both eyes. Both eyes focus on the target, with the master eye in the correct alignment to serve as the gun's rear sight.

Keeping both eyes open while looking down the barrel of a shotgun takes some getting used to, but you'll never be able to consistently hit moving targets with one eye closed. (Some people shoot that way, I know, but none of them shoots very well with that self-imposed handicap.) The great danger for beginners is thinking that they can learn to do this later. But habits are tough to break. It's best to learn to do it correctly from the outset.

How do you pull the trigger? It seems like a picayune concern, but how you pull the trigger can have unfortunate ramifications. Some shooters want to get the entire first joint of their finger beyond the trigger. When the time comes to fire the shotgun, they pull with a "come here" motion. Often, this habit can be traced back to the old clunker they learner to shoot with—a gun that needed a mighty yank to set it off.* That method causes untold trouble with two-trigger shotguns: finger-wrappers find it impossible to quickly switch from one trigger to another. Also, those who claim to be unable to shoot while wearing gloves are most likely members of the trigger-wrapper clan.

Other shooters touch the trigger with just the fingerprint of their index finger. This group has a better feel for the trigger in all situa-

---

* If you find that you really have to "pull" rather than "move" the trigger, a gunsmith can lessen the amount of force needed to release the sear. A heavy or sloppy trigger pull is not the sort of problem you're aware of until it's fixed, and then you wonder how you ever managed to hit anything when you had to yank so hard. According to one of the convoluted laws of shooting, the harder you have to pull on a trigger, the more you tense up and the more you feel the recoil. Lessen the trigger pull, and any gun seems to shoot softer.

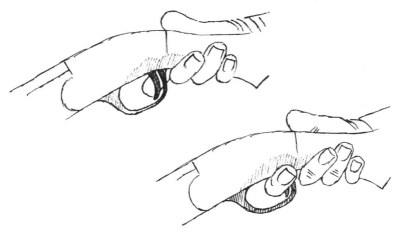

Two methods of pulling the trigger.

tions. It's a fundamental difference. Trigger-yankers have developed a bad habit that they'll want to change someday. If you're starting over, remember that the best way to avoid a bad habit is not to form it in the first place.

Do you fumble with the gun's safety? When hunting, the gun is loaded while you're walking around, so the safety has to be in the "safe" position. Working the safety is one of those things you have to practice until it becomes automatic. It's an exceptional hunting situation that permits time to shift your focus away from the target long enough to look for and find the gun's safety, click it to the "off" position, and then refocus on the target. Remington and a few other companies make a cross-bolt safety that is fairly positive and is operated with the same finger that pulls the trigger, which makes it even safer. Most other safety designs are not planned with ease of operation in mind. It seems that the more expensive the gun, the more inconspicuous the safety. You can't concentrate on a flushing bird and work a safety at the same time if you can't feel it. Oversized safety buttons are sold to replace those installed by the factory. Take the gun to a gunsmith if you don't trust yourself to do a proper job.

If you're serious about becoming a competent field shooter, putting the safety off should be a part of every gun mount. Equally important is putting it back on again after the shot. Double guns, when made as field models, often have an automatic safety* that clicks into the "safe" position when the gun is opened.

How automatic is your reloading move? When I was a teenager, just learning how to shoot my new pump gun, I was having some difficulty. A fellow who I later discovered was a superb wing shot (the late Jimmy Downing, former Massachusetts skeet champion several times over) gave me a piece of advice that went right to the core of my problem. He said, "You've got to think of shucking out the empty and pumping a new round into the chamber as the *completion* of the shot you just took rather than the *beginning* of a new one." His advice made sense to me then, and it still does 50 years later. It was my first introduction to the idea that a complete shot is a lot more than the act of pulling the trigger. For a field shooter, a complete shot has to involve the whole dynamic of mounting the gun, putting off the safety, finding the line, moving the gun, firing, putting the safety back on, and reloading.

Obviously, you can't practice reloading at the range—when your turn to shoot is over, your gun should remain empty. But in the field, an unloaded gun is of no use. You need to get into the habit of reloading the gun quickly, before you take another step. Reloading has to become as automatic as any other part of the process, because there will be times when your attention is elsewhere: the dog is still on point or the covey needs to be marked down or the crippled duck is swimming for the weeds.

My own excuse for not being accomplished at reloading is that grouse are usually found as single birds, as are woodcock. But then I went quail hunting. When chasing bobwhites, there is often one reluctant bird that stays put after the covey has flown off. Taking just one additional step invariably flushes the "sleeper." I can testify that when that late bird takes wing and you're in the process of reloading, all you can do is curse. To guard against such moments, I had my wife sew a pair of shell loops to the outside of my gunning vest so that I can cut down on the time it takes to reload. If I could just permit the ejectors to spit the empties out as they're

---

* Most double guns can be converted to automatic safety. Usually, the necessary channel was cut into the interior of the frame when the gun was made. A clever gunsmith can add the connection rod and retainer with minimal effort and expense.

designed to, I could shave several more seconds off my reloading time. But I can't—I've spent too many years catching the empties and putting them in my vest pocket, and it has become an unbreakable habit when opening the gun.

Adults long out of school routinely undertake new activities or set new goals and actually accomplish them. They quit smoking or lose 20 pounds or learn to play the harmonica. Becoming a good shot is easier

Your reloading move must be automatic.

than any of those. Going back to the title of this chapter: starting over involves shaking whatever bad habits you may have formed, and getting better addresses the creation of new and positive habits. Ideally, your shooting habits should make you a better shot; they shouldn't be something that you shoot well in spite of. If you recognized a bad habit or two of your own, now is the time to correct it.

Learning something new is one thing. Unlearning something wrong and replacing it with a new method takes 6 weeks of attention, by one estimate. (Some of my eggheaded friends who deal with cerebral issues tell me that there is something called "reactive inhibition" that fights the whole process.) I call this "starting over," because shaking those bad habits will take some surrender, and you might feel like a beginner again for a while. On the road to becoming a good shot, the potholes and washouts that can keep you from moving ahead are called bad habits. You're on that road, and you might need to learn a few new things about gun handling to continue the journey. Gun mount is essential to every upland-shooting situation— you can't do much without mastering that basic technique. The other points mentioned in this chapter don't fall into the make-or-break category. Once you can hit 20 of 25 targets at skeet and can easily get your gun into shooting position when a bird flushes, "getting better" isn't about doing something a lot better. Rather, it's about doing a lot of things just a little better. A famous golfer once said, "The more I practice, the luckier I get." It applies equally to shotgun shooting. There's one more truth that could be added to the dozen listed in chapter 1: improved results predictably follow improved methods.

Having arrived at the end of the chapter on starting over, it seems like a good place for an editorial about gun safety. Since hunting involves carrying a loaded shotgun around for hours at a time, safety has to be a prime concern. Unfortunately, that's not always true. I often see large groups of pheasant hunters—sometimes half a dozen or more. So many people that close together carrying loaded guns makes me very leery. But when I've given voice to my concerns, I've been told that everyone is careful and knows about gun safety. Then, when a bird flushes, everyone in the line fires until his gun is empty. Why should I believe that any of the assembled multitude knows anything about shotguns other than how to pull the trigger?

In 40 years afield, I've been shot at a dozen times or so, almost always inaccurately. However, I've got a scar on my neck from a pellet of number 4 shot. It came from a shot fired at a distance that everyone agreed was out of range. Twice I've been in the presence of other people who were struck with pellets that broke their skin, and I've seen the aftereffects of a man hit fully with an express load of number 5s at 25 yards. It all hurts like hell, and for a long, long time.

I was standing behind a man when he blew up an expensive shotgun because a piece of cleaning rag was lodged in the barrel, and I was with another who continually tried to load both 12s and 20s into the same gun. I know of two men who unintentionally shot their own bird dogs, and one who sunk a duck boat while he was in it. Another guy shot the heel off his partner's boot. None of it was ever done on purpose, but every incident was a direct result of carelessness.

When I think of the stupidest things I've ever done in my life, every one of them occurred when I was in the presence of several other boys or young men. Now that I'm old doesn't automatically mean that I'm smart, but I've observed that when men-who-used-to-be-boys get together, quite often their maturity takes a step backward and their collective bravado precipitates a form of group recklessness. In every war that's ever been fought with guns, a large percentage of the casualties were the result of recklessness among soldiers on the same side.

At the target range, I don't want to be in the same time zone as anyone who is casual about gun safety. While shooting sporting clays, I have raised my voice to men who were preloading their guns on the way to the station, and I have walked off the range when experienced shooters became a little too cavalier about gun handling because the targets weren't breaking for them. Practices such as "backing up another's shot" are just excuses for fooling around, and that always leads to trouble when loaded guns and men-who-used-to-be-boys come together.

Perhaps the greatest lesson in gun safety is to stay away from dangerous situations in the first place. Vice President Dick Cheney's famous hunting accident was a direct result of far too many hunters on the same field. I want nothing to do with hunting in a group. In my narrow definition, two's company and three's a group. My refusal is based not only on my fear of the other guy's carelessness but also on the possibility of my making a mistake. If I'm hunting with you, stay away from me while my gun is loaded. As careful as I try to be, I know that I'm every bit as capable of inattention as the next guy, and the absolute worst day of my life would be the day I accidentally hurt someone.

The Field Shotgun

When Lance Armstrong titled his autobiography *It's Not about the Bike*, his implication was that success in cycling involves strength and conditioning rather than just having the latest high-tech equipment. And I'd be the first to agree with him: having a bike just like Lance's won't make you win the Tour de France. Similarly, people want to know what kind of gun Joe So-and-so used to win the National Sporting Clays Championship. But it's not about the bike. The gun you use is no more responsible for your misses than it is for your hits—all the credit and blame goes to you, the shooter.

Still, Lance Armstrong wasn't climbing the French Alps on my old rusty Columbia coaster-brake bike. The old beat-up piece of junk I rode to deliver newspapers back when I was a kid served its purpose, but I wouldn't want to enter a race with it. So maybe, in a way, it is partially about the bike (and the gun) after all.

Significant advancements have been made in shotguns in the past 20 years—real improvements that can help you shoot better. In your quest to become a good shot, what kind of "bike" are you using? Are you shooting the old shotgun you inherited from Uncle Ralph? Are you still using the same gun you learned to shoot with 20 years ago? Loyalty is a virtue, but sooner or later you're going to pick up another shooter's shotgun and realize that you can do a lot better than Uncle Ralph's Old Betsey.

If you want to become a good shot, your shotgun should be a lot more than just your handicap weight. Even if the gun isn't going to make you a better shot, it certainly shouldn't work in the opposite direction—you shouldn't have to become a good shot *in spite of* the gun you're using.

I'm not fool enough to tell you which gun to use. You wouldn't listen to me even if I did. But when you decide that it's time for a new gun, it's not enough to just want "something better." Guns cost too much money to keep buying new ones until you happen to find the right one. (For that matter, how many of us would know the "right one" if it was handed to us?) Instead, be methodical about your choice. The list of prerequisites for a field gun is relatively brief. Here's mine:

1. The gun must not have excess weight.
2. The gun must be balanced so that it's easy to carry properly.
3. The gun must be dynamic at the shoulder.
4. The gun must fit the shooter.
5. The gun must produce enough firepower to do the job.
6. The gun must not be so expensive that you're afraid to take it hunting.
7. The gun must be easy to care for.

Just seven items. If you're starting over and looking for a gun to accompany you on the journey to becoming a good shot—or even if you want to justify keeping the gun you have now—this short list is a good point of departure. Let me discuss each item on the list and tell you why it's important.

WEIGHT

Although he was writing almost 70 years ago, William Harnden Foster described the perfect field gun this way: "The ideal grouse gun may be defined broadly as the one that a certain hunter will find most pleasant to carry to the spot where a grouse is to be shot at, and there prove most efficient when the shot is made."[*] A salient point in his somewhat stilted definition is that the carrying part comes first. Unlike target shooting, hunting requires a lot of gun carrying between shots. When there are no birds in the air (which is 99 percent

---

[*] William Harnden Foster, *New England Grouse Shooting* (Scribner, 1942), 91.

of the time), the shotgun is your handicap weight—a burden to be borne while taking a walk outdoors. The more the gun weighs, the more likely it is to tire you out. That said, you might assume that the lighter the gun, the better it is. Unfortunately, the lightest shotgun you can find is not necessarily the lightest gun you can shoot well. Guns that are too light—usually by virtue of being too small—don't swing properly. Then there's the fact that a too-small gun won't be a good fit and might kick the daylights out of you with ordinary loads.

A relevant point in any discussion of the weight of a shotgun is this reminder from Isaac Newton: all recoil is a function of three numbers—the weight (actually, *mass* is the correct term) of the gun, the weight of the shot, and the speed of that shot leaving the gun (that is, the muzzle velocity). It's true that you could shoot a super-duper 2-ounce, 3½-inch, high-velocity magnum load out of a shotgun and never mind the recoil—true, that is, if the gun weighed 14 pounds. Other factors often cited in recoil—chamber pressure, type of wad, recoil pad, amount of choke—are important to other aspects of shooting but not to the reactive force that is recoil.* For now, it's enough to realize that although lightweight guns are the "most pleasant to carry," when it's time to shoot, heavier guns are preferable.

There has to be a compromise—or, in this case, an application of common sense—when it comes to the pairing of gun weight and ammunition. Balance and weight distribution are critical factors in a field gun, but the fact remains that you have to carry the gun for as long as you're hunting. Weight counts for a great deal, so the key is to identify what constitutes *excess* weight. Here are some things to consider:

• A 12-gauge gun loaded with five express loads weighs fully half a pound more than it does when empty.

• In a double-barrel gun, 28-inch barrels weigh a quarter pound more than 26s.

• Smaller-gauge guns naturally have lighter-weight barrels, but they aren't always built on smaller frames, resulting in less weight

---

*The springs involved in an autoloader's action store some of that recoil energy (very briefly). The shooter feels it less because the force is spread out over a longer time. Nevertheless, the shooter's body receives the same total amount of recoil energy.

reduction than might be expected. In many small-gauge repeaters, most of their parts are interchangeable with a 12-gauge.

- Do you need more than two shots? If so, are you willing to carry around the mechanism for reloading the gun? Doubles, of course, have an extra barrel, but automatics routinely weigh a pound more than comparable doubles, all because of the magazine and the sliding machinery needed to extract empties and feed fresh shells into the chamber.

- Lightweight guns are being made with aluminum-alloy receivers and frames, reducing the weight by as much as 1½ pounds.

- You can remove as much as half a pound from a butt stock by drilling away some of the interior wood. The density of the wood is also a factor: fancy wood is heavy. Some companies have been using something that looks suspiciously like mahogany on their gun stocks, but it is light enough to make a considerable difference in the overall weight of the shotgun.

- Beavertail fore-ends add weight. So do ventilated ribs, poly-chokes, palm swell grips, cheek pieces, and recoil pads. It's not much, but anything you add to a shotgun contributes to its overall weight.

None of these points is a consideration if you're not going to be carrying the gun much, such as a duck gun or one intended for target shooting. But if you're going to be spending the day afield with the gun at port arms, you'd be wise to consider how much those three extra shells in the magazine are costing you.

STATIC BALANCE FOR CARRYING

What makes a *well-balanced* shotgun? That term is always being thrown around in gun articles, but it's seldom defined. Without getting too technical, you need to understand that there are two versions of balance as it applies to shotguns. *Static balance* makes the gun easy to carry, and *dynamic balance* makes it easy to mount and shoot (more on dynamic balance later).

As far as carrying goes, a well-balanced gun is one that is most comfortable to carry with your hands in the position they will take when shooting. Since your trigger hand has to go on the grip, balance is pretty much a function of where your left hand is most comfortable. You can get an inkling while handling the gun at the store,

and you might get a feel for it on the skeet range, but to know for sure, you have to take the gun for a walk. Ten minutes later, look at your left hand: if it's right where it needs to be when you throw the gun up for a snap shot, you've got a well-balanced gun.

The accompanying illustrations show the static balance point of two shotguns: my father's old Remington Model 11, which I learned to shoot with 50 years ago, and my current field gun, a Beretta 12-gauge Ultralight. In each illustration, the second triangle represents the change in balance point when the gun is loaded. There is a forward shift in balance when the Remington is loaded with a shell in the chamber and four shells in the magazine, and there is a slight rearward shift of the balance point when the over-under is loaded.

The gun can be thought of as a seesaw, with your trigger hand supporting some of the weight at a given distance from the pivot point. The one correct position for the forward hand is a function of the weight distribution along the length of the shotgun—on a seesaw, a little kid can "outweigh" his bigger friend if he sits far enough away.

Balance points of two guns,
loaded and unloaded.

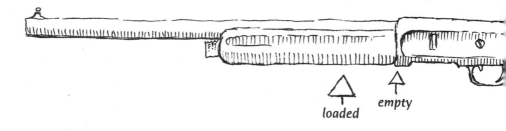

loaded   empty

A gun with the static balance point close to the trigger hand—such as the Beretta Ultralight—is easy to manage when carrying. The back hand takes all the weight of the gun whenever you release your forward hold to push branches out of the way or adjust your hat or any of the other thousand reasons you end up one-handing the gun during a day afield. The farther the distance between the trigger hand and the balance point, the greater the leveraged strain your right wrist has to endure at such times.

Most repeater-style shotguns (that is, pumps and automatics) are easy to shoot but tough to carry because they have a natural weight-forward design. With the length of the receiver inserted between the butt stock and the barrels, the balance point is much farther forward than with double guns. With guns like my father's Model 11, the front hand tries to find the right place on the seesaw to balance the gun while carrying, but that one right spot is at odds with where the hand should be when the gun is mounted. The carried gun becomes a cantilevered weight that keeps trying to fall forward, resulting in a subtle but constant wrestling match that can tire us out far more than

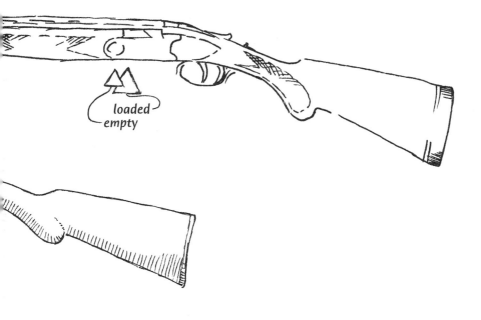

loaded
empty

just the weight of the gun might be expected to. In this case, putting more weight in the stock makes it heavier, but it can also shift the balance point closer to the trigger hand, making the gun a lot easier to carry.

One of the best compliments I've ever heard one shooter pay another involved two friends of mine, both bird hunters. "No matter what time of the day it is," one said of his colleague, "whenever I look his way, he's carrying his gun at high port." That tribute doesn't mean much to someone who isn't a hunter, but the rest of us know what a tip of the hat it really is. And it speaks volumes to the importance of carrying a well-balanced shotgun.

DYNAMIC BALANCE FOR SHOOTING

Birds in flight can be very uncooperative when you're trying to shoot them—they never seem to fly in straight lines or do anything predictable. Bringing a shotgun to your shoulder and swinging it after an unpredictable flying target involves dynamics, and to get those forces to work in your favor (rather than having to overcome them), it is imperative that the gun lend itself to responsive movement. Here's where dynamic balance comes into play.

Rather than getting into a discussion of physics and using scary terms like *moment of inertia, vectors of force,* and *length of righting arm,* I'll make this comparison: Imagine two guns. The first, "Mister Centerweight," is of standard design, with relatively short barrels, and some of the interior wood has been removed from the butt stock. The second gun, "Old Hourglass," has a lightweight frame but longer barrels, and the butt stock is of solid wood. Whether they're repeaters or doubles doesn't matter here. For the sake of argument, let's assume that both guns weigh exactly the same and have exactly the same fulcrum point of static balance.

When a shooter holds Mister Centerweight in a standard manner, most of the gun's weight is concentrated between the shooter's hands. To use the seesaw comparison again, the kids that make up the balance weights are sitting close to the center. Old Hourglass is just the opposite—although balanced, much of the gun's weight is out beyond the natural hand-hold points of the shooter. On the seesaw, the kids are sitting out near the far ends. The state of balance is

"Old Hourglass" and "Mister Centerweight."

the same, but since the kids are farther apart, the seesaw is easier to upset and more difficult to control.

Mister Centerweight, with the weight between the shooter's hands, tends to come up quickly and move easily to the target. The gun is easy to manage while carrying, and one-handing it is easy. If you're going to have trouble with this sort of gun, it will likely be because it doesn't swing as fluidly as you'd like—detractors might say the gun is "muzzle light." As smoothly as it mounts, it can be jittery when tracking the target.

Old Hourglass tends to take a bit more effort to get mounted, but once it's put into motion, it swings more easily. This gun tracks well and swings smoothly, but it isn't as responsive to midswing adjustments as the first. It doesn't carry well, since any momentary letting go with one hand results in a leveraged upsetting force from all that weight out front. When it becomes necessary to one-hand this gun, it's usually so uncomfortable that you'll automatically rest it back on your shoulder.

One-handing it.

Neither gun is right or wrong. Both have their uses, depending on the type of shooting to be done. And, for the sake of illustration, I've described both guns in extreme terms. In truth, Mister Centerweight isn't jittery; it just swings a little less smoothly than the other gun. And Old Hourglass isn't difficult to mount; it just doesn't move as fluidly as Mister Centerweight. The differences are noticeable only in comparison.

Dynamic balance is a subjective term. It can't be measured in the same manner as length of pull or overall weight. A shotgun that might be considered dynamically balanced for an average-size shooter might be clumsy for a shorter person or too whippy for someone taller and stronger. It's a judgment you've got to make for yourself.

Target guns are designed to be of the Old Hourglass type—that is, weight-forward or muzzle-heavy. At skeet shoots, you might routinely see shooters with snap-on weights added to the barrels of their shotguns. They're certainly not added to make the gun lighter or prettier. Guns designed for waterfowl hunting are of a similar weight-forward design. You don't do a lot of carrying of either type gun—at least not in the ready-to-shoot posture. The weight-forward design indicates that the shooter's chief concern is that the gun swings smoothly. This attribute is accomplished at the expense of dynamic balance. That doesn't make them bad guns, but rather, special-purpose guns suited to a particular type of shooting where gun mount can be accomplished ahead of time. For upland bird hunting, guns of the Mister Centerweight type—with most of the gun's weight between the shooter's hands—are the most responsive.

FIT

Guns can fit you either well or improperly, but there is a definite "human scale" that is part of each shotgun's design. Since humans come in a wide variety of shapes and sizes, you might think that shotguns would too, but just about every gun that's made today comes in a one-size-fits-all sort of nonsize. Fortunately, most guns fit most people.

To repeat what I said earlier, there is only one proper position in which a shotgun can be fired accurately. To be aimed (in the general manner that shotguns are aimed), a shotgun must fit into the correct alignment of gun butt–to–shoulder pocket and cheek-to-comb, so that the eye of the shooter is looking right down the barrel's rib. In that position, the forward hand is supporting some of the gun's weight and actively pinching the remainder back against the shoulder pocket. The trigger hand supports none of the weight. The whole arrangement of limbs, head, shoulder, and shotgun is known in this book as the "tangled knot." As you move the gun, the tangled knot

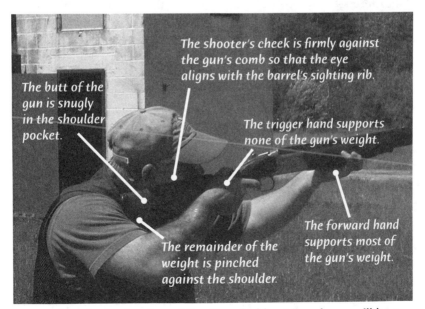

The shooter's cheek is firmly against the gun's comb so that the eye aligns with the barrel's sighting rib.

The butt of the gun is snugly in the shoulder pocket.

The trigger hand supports none of the gun's weight.

The remainder of the weight is pinched against the shoulder.

The forward hand supports most of the gun's weight.

Remember the intricacies of the "tangled knot," and you will be a better shooter.

is easily "untied" unless proper attention is paid to its preservation (see chapter 3).

Guns are made to fit humans, but humans can adjust to fit guns, too. That some people can accurately and routinely shoot shotguns of various designs and dimensions is testimony to the human ability to adjust. Even so, it's nice to pick up a shotgun and have it fit like Cinderella's slipper—the gun effortlessly finds its way into the middle of the tangled knot and, without a thought, it's pointing where you're looking. (To complete the Cinderella analogy, you fall in love and marry the shotgun, never miss another shot, and live happily ever after.)

For many of us, however, a bit of alteration is necessary before the gun fits like the glass slipper. A recoil pad can add some length to the stock, which is often the only adjustment tall people need. Anything more than that requires a stock fitter, and unless you have your own team of expert gunsmiths on retainer, that can become semi-expensive. Nevertheless, these costly little adjustments can make all the difference in the world. Alterations to the drop of the stock or to the gun's pitch—that is, the angle at which the butt plate meets your shoulder—are relatively easy. Such adjustments can change the way your eye lines up with the barrel of the gun and also change the way you feel the gun's recoil. Weight can be added (very easily) or subtracted (not so easily) to affect the gun's balance point, which in turn affects the way you mount the gun and, ultimately, how the gun fits in that all-important moment when it hits your shoulder.

Recoil is always a problem with guns that don't fit. When properly aligned, the gun's recoil comes straight back and is absorbed by the mass of your body through the butt of the gun. The gun should sit squarely in the pocket made at your shoulder when your trigger hand reaches forward. With an improper fit, the gun delivers its recoil at a vector other than straight back, smacking your face and pulling the gun out of your hands. Heavy loads take a lot of the blame for recoil problems, but in truth, people who get beat up by shotguns are usually shooting one that doesn't fit.

Some people are afraid that making any alteration will diminish the resale value of the gun, so that they won't add a recoil pad or alter the safety button. This fear seems to possess many owners of ordinary factory guns. Make up your mind as to just who owns your shotgun. If your gun needs a stock alteration, you should do it—to heck with the next buyer. I've seen people using black electrician's tape to hold a recoil pad or a palm swell in place because they're afraid to "spoil" the looks of the gun permanently. When I'm feeling sarcastic, I usually compliment them on a nice tape job.

Here's another stupid idea: "A field gun should shoot slightly high, since most shots will be taken at rising birds." That's a quote you can find in bad articles about field shooting, and I couldn't disagree more. If you want to become a wing shot, you need a gun that will shoot where you point it. You can't learn to hit a rising target with a gun designed to cover your mistakes. Such a high-shooting gun will work against the shooter in every situation other than the one-and-only situation it's designed for. Save the high-shooting guns for the trap field, where the rising aspect of every shot is predictable.

Since the gun is a dynamic tool, every change will affect everything else. Adding or subtracting anything to a gun—even something as mundane as loading it—affects its balance, both static and dynamic. When it comes to changes, go slowly.

Then there is the lesson of the Havilah Babcock story. (I've heard it retold in several ways, but I think his version titled "The Fallen Lady" is the original.) In a pinch, Babcock borrowed an old beat-up shotgun from a tenant farmer and found that he couldn't miss with it. He bought the gun, then discovered that the barrels were Damascus steel. He was afraid to continue using the gun, but he spared no expense in having a new gun custom-made to the identical dimensions and weight. Of course, it wasn't the same. It never is. All guns have a bit of individuality, and they are much more than the sum of their dimensions. I know for sure that the dimensions on my overunder double would result in a very different gun when applied to a side-by-side and another altogether different gun when applied to an autoloader. They would all have the same length of pull, same drop at comb, same weight, and so forth, but they would be three very different guns.

I like to quote George Bird Evans on shotgun fit: "With a gun made to fit you like prescription glasses, all you have to do is learn where to look." That sums it up. But, of course, you still have to know where to look and how to go about that act of looking. A well-fitting shotgun doesn't automatically make you a good shot. It is, however, a factor in your favor.

FIREPOWER

The job of a field shotgun is to cleanly kill a gamebird, as opposed to breaking a clay target. The two should never be confused, but they often are. Targets in flight need only be hit to be broken, but to be killed instantly and consistently (rather than just knocked down or killed some of the time), gamebirds need a much more powerful knockout blow. There is a whole magnitude of difference between the two requirements, and a field gun should be selected with that difference in mind.

"Use enough gun" is an oft-repeated motto. Some shooters who should know better think that the only difference among gauges is the amount of shot that comes out the end of the barrel. That's not true. Gauge matters. Larger-gauge guns are more efficient than smaller gauges and can be counted on to deliver a similar amount of shot in a much more deadly manner. The whys and wherefores of that phenomenon are discussed in chapter 6, but for now, it's enough to say that smaller-gauge guns may produce lovely patterns with fine shot, but they progressively lose their efficiency as the shot size grows more coarse.

The 20-gauge is a good upland gun that can handle number 6 shot well, but it can be pushed to ridiculous extremes by those who think they need to shoot 3-inch shells out of a bore designed to efficiently handle a little less than an ounce of shot. These individuals have a foot in each camp—they are enamored with the reduced weight of the 20, but they can't come to terms with the idea that such a gun might be able to do the job with less than 12-gauge performance. With the exception of waterfowl and turkeys, the 20 will produce enough firepower—with standard loads—to do just about anything you could ask of it.

There are few things the 16-gauge can't do, but it was left behind 80 years ago when the skeet shooting community failed to recognize it as a separate and bona fide classification. There are separate events for the 20, the 28, and the .410, but anyone who shows up with a

16-gauge is lumped in with the 12s. For its part, the 16-gauge never fought back—nobody ever invented a 3-inch magnum for the 16, specialty loads for the gauge don't exist, and the 16 is absent from most gun catalogs today. There is a small group of sportsmen who continue to promote the "sweet 16." They are willing to put up with the drawbacks of using an obsolete gun in order to shoot the same thing their grandfathers shot. Good for them. At least they've got a reason for putting themselves through the wringer.

The 28-gauge has become the darling of gun writers. The terms *lightweight* and *fast-handling* are universally used to describe the gun, and its proponents claim a near-mystic ability to do things with ¾ ounce of shot that bigger guns do with more. Unfortunately, what they don't tell you is that the 28-gauge won't handle anything larger than number 7½ shot very efficiently.

When it comes to small-gauge guns—the 20 and the 28—consider that the killing power of any load is a direct function of the weight of that charge. This means that 1⅛ ounces of shot is better than a 1-ounce load, and 1 ounce trumps a lighter load every time. In woodland hunting situations, part of the gun's pattern is routinely absorbed by intervening brush and branches before it reaches the target. If a brush hunter believes in the killing power equation, it makes sense to put as much shot into the pattern as feasible to off-set the loss. In contrast, when shooting small birds in open country (bobwhites, Huns, chukars, doves, desert quail), a smaller-gauge gun might provide all the firepower you need.

My objection to the .410 is that it is a proven crippler. I've seen dozens of .410 patterns and have yet to view one that I thought was fit to shoot at a gamebird. The patterns are so inconsistent that you can be right on a bird (or a target) and still not hit it. A miss with the .410 doesn't automatically equate to a mistake and thus a lesson, yet adults continue to put .410s in the hands of children on the mis-guided assumption that it's a good "beginner's gun."

A stumbling point on the firepower issue is some people's inter-pretation of sportsmanship. The idea that using light loads or small-gauge guns gives the bird a "sporting chance" has never made a lot of sense to me. Hunting was never intended to be fair. It's not one golfer competing against another on a level playing field—it's a human being killing an animal. In hunting, the "sporting chance" idea is laudable right up to the time the hunter mounts the gun. After that, fairness and good sportsmanship amount to doing a thorough job of killing the bird. To me, that means maximizing the pattern so that the bird is hit hard with a big load of shot from a big gun. Some people have a cavalier attitude about it all—they can kill quail with a .410 or shoot a goose in the head with a 28-gauge. Of course, it can be done—sometimes. But in shotgunning, the only measure of effectiveness is consistency. When hunting, respect for the gamebird amounts to ensuring a clean and instantaneous kill. A feathered bird that flies off with a couple pellets in its body hasn't been given a sporting chance; rather, it has received a death sentence. Some wounded birds survive, but most don't.

Before leaving the firepower issue, consider the following: Through the first 35 years of my adult life, I shot various 20-gauge guns at everything that flew in the uplands. I believed that the 20-gauge was as deadly a gun as I needed. But I'm compulsive about keeping records, and those shooting journals showed that no matter how carefully I selected my shots, I couldn't kill cleanly more than 65 percent of the birds I hit with the 20-gauge. I switched to a 12-gauge gun in 1999, and my clean-kill record has moved into the 75 percent range. I don't hit *more* birds with the 12-gauge, but I kill cleanly more of the birds I hit. You won't notice the difference between a 65 percent and a 75 percent clean-kill rate unless you keep records. Will it matter on your next shot? Probably not. But if you keep track of such things, the difference will definitely show up over the course of a season.

EXPENSE

I used to go to sea with a fellow whose motto in life was: "Money is no problem—I don't have any." Similarly, for many of us, a too-expensive gun is hardly worth worrying about. The standard American shotgun has always cost the standard American worker a week's pay. That was true back when the standard was the Browning Auto-5, and it was true in the second half of the twentieth century when the Remington 1100 took its place. There have always been cheaper guns available, and, of course, there are finer guns for those who can afford them. But all guns, even the cheap ones, are expensive.

Having said that, I need to add that shotguns are a consumable item, intended to be used and used until they are used up. Some are meant to last a dozen lifetimes, others only one or two, but every gun is eventually going to end up as scrap metal and firewood, so you might as well use it and get your money's worth.

If your shotgun is an investment on which you expect to turn a profit by reselling it sometime in the future, then by all means, don't take it hunting. For that matter, don't even shoot it, because the very act of using a gun results in wear and thus diminishes its value. But if selling the gun is your goal, this isn't the gun we should be talking about in a discussion of how to become a good shot. For our purposes, your "best" gun is the one you shoot best, and that's the one you should be using in the field.

Lovely as they are, fancy wood, elaborate checkering, and fine engraving are liabilities on a shotgun intended for hunting. You don't need any of that, and it drives up the price without making the gun shoot one iota better. But any gun can fall into the "too-expensive" category if you're afraid that using it in the uplands will scratch the finish or that salt water will damage the bluing. I don't mean to champion carelessness, but it seems that the people who are most afraid of what the elements will do to their shotguns are the ones who have the least idea what to do about it—how to minimize the effects in the first place, and how to properly treat a gun that has spent time afield.

Routine care and preventive maintenance make sense. Don't use the gun as a canoe paddle or a pry bar for lifting rocks. Get a good gun case and use it. Keep a rag and some aerosol gun-juice handy in the car's trunk for wipe-downs as needed. But hunting guns are made to go hunting, and the dings and scratches that result from a season afield are part of the bargain. Be wise: don't get a gun that is so expensive that the first scratch causes Wall Street to shudder.

CARE AND MAINTENANCE

My dad spent the first half of his life shooting an artillery piece that passed itself off as a 12-gauge Remington Model 11. It was all things that old guns are supposed to be: full-choked, heavy, and—in its own way—handsome. There was a patina of honest wear on that old gun; the checkering and the bluing were worn smooth in the right places, and the wood, though perfectly ordinary, had a deep maroon luster that only the years could impart. The handsomeness extended to the internals, where each part was a precision-machined thing of beauty.

But taking the Model 11 apart and putting it back together took a huge amount of skill and labor. It wasn't as complicated as an automatic transmission, but almost. As a result, cleaning the gun was a once-a-year extravaganza that took the better part of an evening at the kitchen table. On all other occasions, my father ran a cleaning rod down the barrel and wiped everything down with gun oil. He knew about gun care from his time as an infantryman, so the oil went onto both metal and wood, and he used lots of it.

With the first paycheck I earned after college, I bought Dad a brand-new Remington automatic. The 1100 was (and still is) an internal-combustion machine—a gas-operated pump gun—with inelegant stamped-out internals. But the charm of a gun that could be field-stripped to its component parts with nothing more than a set of car keys as a tool was not lost on my father. The 1100 was taken apart, cleaned, and put back together after each outing. It took all of 10 minutes. Dad's 1100 was always clean because it was easy to clean. Once a year he took the stock off and regreased the through-bolt and spring, but there wasn't anything complicated about that. Replacement parts, when needed, were easy to obtain. He replaced the return spring and the gas seal O-ring several times as routine maintenance, but the only repair in 35 years was to the ejector, which just wore out with use.

Preventive maintenance for any field gun needs to be routine in every sense of the word. There are lots of fine products out there to protect a shotgun's finish, but they won't work if they're still in the can. If you don't know how to take your gun apart for a yearly internal cleaning, have someone show you how—it's not high science, but it can be daunting to the uninitiated.

Firing pins, hammer springs, and locking lugs are consumable parts of a shotgun. Like the brakes on an automobile, they are designed to absorb wear and eventually need to be replaced. Finishes don't last forever either. After a dozen years of service, it's not unusual for a gun to need rebluing. The same goes for renewing the stock's finish.

But the bottom line is that it should all be easy to do. Dad's 1100 met all the requirements, but the old Model 11 was never routinely clean because it wasn't easy. Make sure you don't fall into that trap.

OTHER CONSIDERATIONS

If you're shopping, you might discover the unfortunate truth that gun manufacturers universally equate "field model" with "economy model." Most field guns are cheap versions of the company's flagship shotguns. That's too bad, because in some ways—particularly weight and balance—a field gun needs to be more exacting than a gun made for target shooting.

Are you prejudiced in favor of or against one particular type of shotgun? Do you consider the 12-gauge a cannon? Or do you think that small-gauge guns are toys? How about automatics? I've heard some people call them contraptions. Those at the other end of the spectrum often refer to double-barrel shotguns—particularly over-and-under shotguns—as fancy or expensive and to those who shoot them as rich or snobby. No less a sportsman than Frank Woolner referred to recoil pads as effeminate. My own father never said the words *ventilated rib* without also using the word *useless*. Such attitudes might be funny, except that they cloud our judgment and keep us from reaching objective conclusions.

"Lock, stock, and barrel" has come to mean "the whole thing." It's an expression left over from a time when guns were simple affairs consisting of those three basic components and were loaded through the business end. Double-barrel shotguns came out of that same era. I once heard someone say of doubles, "If you can close it, you can shoot it." Although that's not necessarily the case, it's true that there are a lot fewer things that can go wrong with a double than with a repeater. Single-trigger mechanisms and automatic ejectors complicate what is still the simplest of shotgun designs. Admittedly, there are plenty of overly long, muzzle-heavy doubles in the gun rack at every sporting clays competition, but when reasonably designed, doubles tend to be close-coupled, weight-centered guns that are comfortable to carry and quick to respond.

Sometimes, with a double gun, just knowing that you've got a long-range choke in the second barrel can provide a comfort factor. When you know that you have a viable backup, you can take the extra moment needed to be sure of your first shot. Nobody has yet invented a self-tightening choke device for single-barrel guns. Until such a contraption hits the market, single-barrel shooters will be limited to repeating the performance level of their first shot each time they pull the trigger.

Factory-made ammunition and repeating shotguns were developed at about the same time, with one making the other possible. The autoloading shotgun—particularly the Browning Auto-5 and its imitators—rose to popularity in the United States during the middle years of the twentieth century. It was a generational thing, spawned by the belief that shotgun shooting was chancy, and the more lead you put out there, the better your chances. By inference, my father's generation didn't expect to make a single accurate shot, but they were fully prepared to keep pulling the trigger until the bird came down.

Just about all gamebirds in the Northeast are taken one at a time, and the opportunity for a shot can come and go so quickly that hunters may wonder why they even bother loading more than one shell. But if you hunt quail or other covey gamebirds, sometimes a gun with more than a double's two shots is welcome. Waterfowlers are often glad to have a third shot to finish off a down-but-not-out duck before it can swim away. I've also shot pheasants in Texas by a method that corralled all the birds in a quarter section of milo stubble into one small corner. When the birds started going up in groups of a dozen or more, suddenly the extra weight of a full magazine didn't seem like such a harebrained idea.

There are some very expensive and exacting shotguns made for the various target games. All target guns are heavy by necessity. A shooter might take more shots in an hour than a hunter takes in a full season afield. Since recoil is a direct function of the weight of the gun, lightweight guns quickly wear out their welcome on any target field. Then, too, there is this salient fact: nobody cares about the carrying weight or balance of a target gun, because they aren't carried—at least, not the way a hunting gun is carried. In all forms of target shooting—skeet, trap, sporting clays, five-stand, FITASC—the gun is loaded on the station only. At all other times it is racked, cased, or opened—and *unloaded*. A target shooter never takes so much as a single step with a loaded gun. Target shooting is only about marksmanship, so in terms of the shotgun, all other considerations are secondary. Target guns aren't bad guns; rather, they are suited for a particular purpose—they are specialists in one type of shooting.

When shopping for a gun, you might look at your purchase as a "lease." Buy a new shotgun, and if you don't like it, resell it 6 months or a year later. Unless you paid the maximum retail price, or unless you beat it up pretty badly, you might lose only a few dollars on the deal. Look at the loss as having rented the gun for a time.

Guns don't routinely wear out, so don't be afraid to buy a secondhand modern gun if you suspect it's what you want. (If you want a particular gun, check the bulletin board at the skeet club every now and then. I have a bunch of shooting acquaintances who change guns the way some men change their socks.) As noted earlier, certain parts of any shotgun are designed to absorb wear and routinely need to be replaced, but beware of the "shot-out" gun that has been used with too-heavy loads and has shocked itself loose. In such a gun, the metal-to-metal fits have been distorted, and the screws that hold the whole thing together are worn out, as are the threads they screw into. There is no easy fix for such a gun, which is best left in the "for sale" rack.

What about old guns? If you're shooting a Remington Model 32 or a vintage Parker that's still tight after a half century or more, I envy you. A few shotguns from my father's generation were ahead of their time, and they remain lithe and dynamic even by today's standards. Unfortunately, those are the exceptions rather than the rule. Most shotguns from my father's generation were routinely choked "full." Back then, people didn't seem to have any problem with the contradictory ideas of pointing dogs and full chokes—a fact that has me scratching my head even now. Mostly, old guns epitomize many of the things we don't want in a shotgun. They are almost always heavier than their modern-day counterparts, replacement parts are often impossible to find, and their design doesn't incorporate the many advances that make modern shotguns modern:

screw-in chokes, gas operation, chrome-lined barrels, tapered forcing cones, fast lock times and easily adjusted triggers, weather-resistant finishes for both metal and wood, lightweight alloy frames and receivers, simple designs, interchangeable components, and ease of maintenance.

To use an analogy: if you were just beginning to take up golf or baseball, no one would expect you to become proficient using the same equipment your grandfather used—old overstuffed fielder's gloves or hickory-shafted persimmon clubs. You can't even sell that old stuff at a garage sale anymore. There have been significant improvements in equipment in the last 50 years, and that goes for shotguns as well. You might do okay with Uncle Ralph's Old Betsey, but it's a foregone conclusion that you'd shoot better with a modern gun.

Still, no one was ever talked out of being in love. Some people genuinely adore old guns—after all, the "sweet 16" didn't get its name because someone thought it was a piece of junk. Sometimes, people invest huge amounts of time and effort into gun restoration projects, and I wouldn't try to persuade them to abandon their pet guns that they restocked and rubbed umpteen coats of True-oil into. But others only think they're in love. In reality, they're just infatuated. They've always wanted a certain type of gun, and now that they can finally afford one, they can't bring themselves to admit that it's not everything they had hoped for. Or, having inherited the very gun that Uncle Ralph used, they find that they can't shoot it. Or maybe they've just gotten used to a particular gun and want to believe that they've made the right choice. Although it's a poor workman who blames his tools, in some cases, poor shooting performance may be related to the old clunker someone is trying to shoot. Loyalty should not be confused with love. Neither should chauvinism or stubbornness.

Traditionalists often fall in love with an ideal rather than reality. Despite the legend that had him married to his gun, if Uncle Ralph could have afforded a better shotgun, he probably would have bought one. Alternatively, if he really was deeply devoted to hunting and shooting, as we imagine him to have been, he would have owned a better gun. Uncle Ralph used what he could afford or, more likely, a gun that was already in the family. Uncle Ralph was never in love with his old clunker—why should you be?

When the time comes for you to replace or improve the shotgun you use for bird hunting, remember that results count. It's easy to become sidetracked by any number of things, including what the gun looks like and the rose-colored image of the gun you imagine yourself shooting. Whatever you select, you're on the road to becoming a good shot, and the gun should further your quest, not hinder it.

The Myth of Inconsistency: Three Solutions

At the skeet range, a fellow chipped a target for a hit. He smiled and said to me, "I'd rather chip 25 straight than smash 24." It was supposed to be a humorous statement—the equivalent of a baseball player getting a bloop hit and saying, "Thank goodness they don't put pictures on the scorecard." But his sentiments revealed that he was not a hunter.

A chipped target and a cleanly killed gamebird should never be confused. When it comes to flying game, the stakes and the standards are higher. In the field, a chipped clay target equates to a down-but-not-out bird or, even worse, a bird that keeps flying. A bird hunter would rather miss cleanly.

Do you have a problem with hitting birds but not killing them outright? Do you "feather" birds that keep flying? Did someone tell you that this is an inevitable part of shotgunning? That sometimes the bird is struck in a less-than-vital area and is destined to be lost? Don't buy into those excuses. None of it has to be true.

We all hit and we all miss, but there is no defense for the in between—that is, a less-than-dead bird. Lost gamebirds are a reality, but put the blame where it belongs: sometimes it's a matter of a rushed shot, an inaccurate shot, or a misjudgment of range. We all try to be good marksmen and keep mistakes to a minimum, but sometimes we fail. That's not the point. The point is that when you make a good shot and still lose the bird, something needs to be corrected, and it's *not* your marksmanship.

Think of skeet: When a target is unbroken after a shot, it's because the shooter missed, plain and simple. Skeet shooters don't blame their misses on the inexactness of shotgunning. They know that the reason for a missed target can be found in their shooting, not their equipment. The same can be said of any of the other target games—a miss is attributable to an error in shooting. If the shooter has been paying attention, it also translates into a lesson. Inconsistency of the pattern doesn't even enter into consideration because it is a nonfactor.*

The "zero tolerance" motto of every corporate safety department needs to be adopted for field shooting as well. Shotgunning is *not* scattergunning—at least not in this century—and it is not unreasonable to expect that birds properly centered in the pattern will be hit hard 100 percent of the time. Shotgun inconsistency is a myth— or at least it can be. If you're willing to do just a little homework, your results can be as predictable as the outcome of a Perry Mason trial. You can guarantee that if you shoot well and cover the bird with the pattern, the bird will be dead in the air every time. The solution is divided into three parts:

1. Putting the shock theory into practice
2. Establishing a slot for your field shooting
3. Adjusting your gun-load-choke combination to changing situations

SHOCK THEORY

A bird in flight is like a delicate airplane—break any bone, and it cannot remain aloft. There are hunters who hang their hats on that statement: knock the bird down, and let the retriever do the rest. A pellet of fine shot usually doesn't pack enough wallop to break a wing bone or penetrate to the bird's vitals, so they elect to use the

---

* The exception is the .410. Patterns are so poor with that gauge that a shooter needs both skill and luck to ever break 25 of 25 at skeet or accomplish anything on a consistent basis.

coarse stuff. They're banking on the idea that with a couple hundred pellets in the air, one of them is bound to hit the target in the right place.

In the opposite corner are the believers in fine shot. They argue that the total hydrostatic shock delivered by many small pellets striking a lightly feathered bird is consistent from shot to shot, and that shock effect alone will kill the bird instantly.

As an aside here: it should be noted that every upland bird falls into the "lightly feathered" category—that is, every kind of grouse, quail, pigeon, prairie chicken, pheasant, chukar, ptarmigan, woodcock, snipe, rail, and dove. In every species, young birds have a thinner feather layer than mature birds, but all are lightly feathered when compared with waterfowl. Ducks and geese have an underlayer of down feathers that acts as a shock-absorbing pad surrounding the bird's body. Compared with upland birds, they're nearly bulletproof. There's a lot to be said for the penetration school of thought when the game involved is waterfowl. Coarse shot has an armor-piercing effect—it holds its shocking power and gets through to the bird's vitals.

When the penetration theory works, the bird dies when hit by three or four big pellets. With luck on the shooter's side, one of those pellets will strike the bird's spine or a vital organ or at least break a bone. When hit in a critical place, the bird dies within 30 seconds. But sometimes the pellets don't strike anything vital, and it might take 30 minutes or longer—it all depends on where the pellets hit the bird and how much physical trauma is done.

With less luck on the shooter's side, the bird is hit, but not fatally so. It may or may not be able to remain in flight—without a broken bone, all birds can "carry shot" and keep going. Good bird dogs can find cripples, but no one should be so naïve as to think that retrieving dogs always succeed. My own setters sometimes pick up crippled birds that have gotten away from other hunters. Usually, the injury that keeps the bird from flying is a single pellet of coarse shot that has struck a nonvital area.

A perfectly round pellet is the best we can get from a shotgun shell, but compared with a spinning bullet, it is a very inefficient projectile, both in flight and when it comes to penetration. When a round lead pellet strikes a bird less than squarely, it tends to change direction and can often be found lodged just under the skin. Such hits deliver shock but do no physical damage to the bird in flight.

Some people use number 6 or 5 shot in woodland situations on the theory that big pellets will blast right through the thick stuff. But I don't know of anyone who has ever put up a pattern sheet on the other side of "the thick stuff" just to see how much of his shot "blasted right through." I suspect the results would be disappointing.

Others use coarse shot in the mistaken belief that a single pellet will bring a bird down. First of all, that's rarely true, no matter how coarse the shot. Second, if they really believe the single-pellet theory, they don't have a clear idea of what they're using their shotguns for. You may remember the time Uncle Ralph dropped a bird at an unbelievable distance, but in truth, even he was surprised when the bird came down. Less memorable—but a much better lesson—would have been if Uncle Ralph had put the gun's safety back on and said, "That's too far. We'll get that one next time."

Coarse shot—that is, number 6, 5, and 4—holds its velocity well, but all patterns thin out at long ranges. Patterns are spotty to begin with when coarse shot is used, and out beyond the effective range of the gun's choke, even a centered bird might be struck by only a single pellet or two. Long-range shooting causes cripples, and coarse shot somehow encourages long-range shooting. In the clay target games, you don't shoot at targets on the next field, so why shoot at birds that are too far away?

It's easy to understand why a bird falls out of the air if a wing is broken, and why it dies if it's hit in the head. But how about the typical 30-yard shot that puts six or seven hits in the body, none of them in a vital area, but the bird is dead just the same? The answer, of course, involves shock.

If you've played baseball, you know how to hit a fungo: with the bat in one hand, you toss the ball up with the other and then make a two-handed swing as the ball falls. If you could squarely hit a crossing pheasant with a line-drive fungo, the bird would be killed instantly. The ball wouldn't have to hit a vital organ or break a bone—it wouldn't even have to break the skin. Transfer enough energy into the bird, and it dies. That's how shock works.

Shocking power is equal to mass *times* velocity, not *plus* velocity. A baseball doesn't travel very fast compared with a load of number 7½ shot, but it has a lot of mass and would produce a very dead pheasant. Likewise, when several pellets strike at the same time, forces are multiplied rather than added. That's the essence of the argument for short shot strings: it's not a matter of hitting the bird with more pellets; rather, it's having all the pellets strike at the same time and multiplying the shock effect. The guarantee of the shock theory is an instantaneous kill 100 percent of the time. When the bird is in range, you don't have to be lucky and hit it in the right place— you just have to hit it.

No matter what load you're using—coarse shot or fine—if enough pellets strike the bird all at once, the hit will transfer sufficient energy to kill the bird instantly. Indeed, when coarse shot produces an instantaneous kill, it's almost always the (incidental) result of the hydrostatic shock effect. But because coarse shot patterns are so irregular, that's not the sort of thing you can rely on. And, as with all things pertaining to shotgunning, reliability is what you're after. Fine shot produces better patterns—denser, more uniform, more efficient. But fine shot quickly loses its shocking power with distance, so the bird has to be in range for the guarantee to be in effect. "Stretching the barrel" is not allowed—which leads right into the next topic.

THE SLOT

After even a short time at the game, shooters instinctively know when they're "on" and when they're not. When you make what seems like a good shot, you expect the bird to be hit hard, but that's not always the case. Why? One answer is that maybe you have an incorrect impression of the pattern and how it is distributed. Unfortunately, you're up against the invisibility factor again: since you can't actually see what's going on out there, the results don't necessarily lead to good conclusions.

The next step along the road to becoming a good shot is getting acquainted with how your shotgun delivers a load of shot throughout its effective range. That involves patterning your shotgun. By this, I don't mean just shooting at a cardboard box (all you learn from this is that shotgun pellets go right through cardboard, and there's a heck of a lot of them. I hope that's not news to anyone.) To do it right, you need to be a bit of a scientist about it. The patterns you produce will be a snapshot of an otherwise invisible process. It's like an x-ray of something you normally can't see. But you've got to actually take the x-ray and then (this is the important part) believe what you see.

Skeet shooters strive to break the target over the center stake 23 yards away, so skeet chokes have been painstakingly developed to throw near-perfect 30-inch patterns with number 9 shot at exactly that distance. It is understood that patterns will be less perfect at distances other than the 23-yard ideal. In the field, of course, ranges are variable, and real birds don't follow predictable flight paths. Still, if you've hunted, it's usually possible to estimate the general range at which the vast majority of your shots take place. A good approach is to work with a minimum and maximum pair of distances that define a zone. For instance, a pheasant hunter with a flushing dog might find that he doesn't see shots closer than 25 yards, and by the time the bird gets out beyond 35 yards or so, he is either done shooting or, if he has a double-barrel gun, he's using his tighter-choked barrel. His slot would be that 25- to 35-yard zone.

When assessing your own normal range, it's dangerous to dwell on that one spectacular 45-yard bird that crossed in the open, while forgetting the bunch of routine shots that were closer but less memorable. Bad decisions follow. What you're after is the 10-yard zone that defines the range where 90 percent of your opportunities present themselves. That represents the slot where most of your shooting is done.

When patterning, you're interested in discovering the right choke and load to deliver a killing pattern all through the 10-yard range described by your slot. For the pheasant hunter above, he's looking to produce a solid circle of evenly spaced hits at 25 yards. Out at 35 yards, the same pattern should still be sufficiently dense to do the job. (It's unreasonable to expect any shotgun to deliver an effective and predictable pattern across a swath of greater than 30 feet or so, thus the 10-yard zone.) Our pheasant hunter might have to do a little

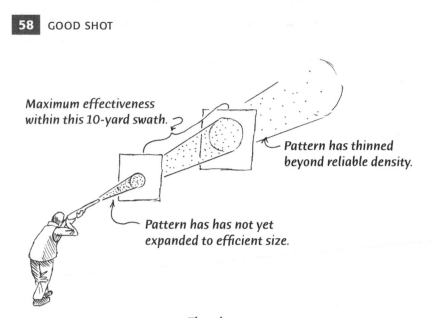

Maximum effectiveness within this 10-yard swath.

Pattern has thinned beyond reliable density.

Pattern has has not yet expanded to efficient size.

The slot.

experimenting with his screw-in chokes and various loads to come up with the right combination, but it exists. The only true measure of a shotgun's effectiveness is consistency. Finding your own right combination will guarantee that a rooster placed in the middle of the pattern, anywhere within your slot, will be hard hit every time.

In my own case, grouse and woodcock hunting is done in coverts, where the bird is often out of sight at 40 yards. New England bird hunting is a short-range affair. With the use of two chokes in an over-under, I've figured my own slot in the grouse coverts to be 17 to 27 yards with the first barrel and 23 to 33 yards with the second. (That point-blank minimum of 17 yards equates to 50 feet, which is about as close as I care to shoot. The 33-yard maximum of the tight barrel is a 100-foot shot.)

In experimenting with the number 8 field load I favor, I found that a straight cylinder produces a lovely entry pattern at 17 yards, but the exit pattern taken 10 yards farther downrange is too thin. The slight choke that is "skeet" is a bit tight at the entry end of the slot but holds together nicely out at the 27-yard exit of the slot, and that is my choice in the open barrel. Improved cylinder choke produces ideal patterns throughout the 23- to 33-yard slot from the top barrel.

To do your own patterning, you'll need to invest in some big sheets of heavyweight paper—something bigger than the 30 inches normally required for a pattern. The paper needs to be oversized because it's important to know what's going on *outside* your effective pattern as well as inside. How much play do you have? What's the margin for error? You can purchase a roll of 48-inch-wide Kraft paper

Entry and exit patterns: the slot of the author's grouse gun.

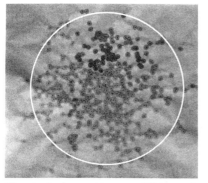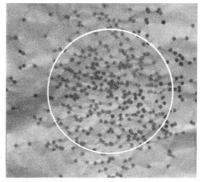

Skeet choke patterns with number 8 shot at the entry (17 yards) and exit (27 yards): a bit tight at entry, but otherwise ideal for close work on grouse and woodcock.

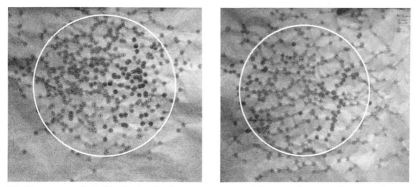

IC (Improved Cylinder) choke patterns with number 8 shot at the entry (23 yards) and exit (33 yards): near perfect patterns made possible by moderate velocity.

for less than $50, or you might be able to pick up some extra-wide sheets at a copy store that reproduces blueprints. Some of my friends use rolls of disposable picnic table covering or the paper used to underlay flooring. Whatever you use, it's got to be big enough to take the whole pattern and then some.

You also need to find a place to actually do the patterning—an abandoned barn or an old fence (with nothing immediately behind it, of course) where you can staple up your pattern sheets. Then you need to do some accurate measuring of the range at which you'll be shooting. If you want to compare one pattern with another, the distances must be consistent and accurate. Patterns taken at "about 30 paces" lose some of their meaning when compared with other patterns taken at a similarly general distance.

Every good pattern produces a "killing circle." The acceptable diameter of the killing circle is up to you. The customary standard is 30 inches, but because the shot swarm expands as it travels, the pattern will be larger—and the pellets spread more thinly—10 yards farther downrange. There's nothing wrong with settling for a 28-inch or even a 26-inch circle at the near end of the slot and one that's a little over 30 inches at the exit end, provided there is sufficient density inside the killing circle.

Evenness of pellet distribution is paramount. It's not just a matter of holes in the pattern that a bird might fly through (although these aren't good news either). Rather, be suspicious of raggedness— bunches of pellet holes with lots of space between them. Such a poor pattern is bound to produce inconsistent results. In field shooting, you'll never know whether the bird will be struck by an unpredictable group of a dozen pellets or whether it will find itself in the thin area right next to it. Considerations such as size of the spread, effective percentage of the load, center weighting, and pellet count are all useful from a comparison standpoint, but evenness of pellet distribution trumps everything.

Patterns are never cookie-cutter neat—the boundaries are vague at best. You need to subjectively define the edge of the effective area: is it a little too small at 25 inches, or too big at 35? Consider, too, that the outer 4 inches of a 30-inch circle contain one-half its area. Realistically, this means that there has to be some overlap if half the effective pattern is to be spread around the rim of the circle. After looking at a few of your own patterns, you'll be able to recognize where they start and stop. Back at home, highlight each pellet hit with a marker so they'll be easier to see.*

I don't mean to suggest that pattern improvement is an end in itself. Don't lose sight of the real reason you're ruining sheet after sheet of perfectly good paper by peppering it full of holes—it's all about what a good pattern translates into in the field. You might find that your patterns are too tight or too big or too ragged. Here are some general rules for improvement:

- Fine shot always patterns better than coarse shot.
- Bigger guns pattern better than smaller gauges.
- Pattern quality is universally improved by reducing muzzle velocity. Being a reloader, I routinely find that even a grain of powder less—something that equates to only 50 feet per second of muzzle velocity—produces better results, sometimes remarkably so.
- Premium quality ammunition always patterns better than the cheap stuff, mostly because the shot itself is harder and less prone to distortion.
- Shot buffer really works. The coarser the shot, the more pronounced its positive effect (more on this later).
- The shot swarm makes a trumpet-shaped expansion as it travels. As a result, even distribution is easy to obtain in close, but distance makes patterns ragged.
- Choke is a mechanical upsetting of the shot stream. More choke equates with more upsetting, and although the pattern will be tighter, there will be a greater percentage of pellets outside the effective area.

---

* I employ a time-consuming but highly illustrative method of examining pattern results. I use a homemade rubber stamp to mark a 1-inch disc around each pellet hole. Somehow, that method appeals to the eye and is easier than attempting to assess a swarm of dots. When I tried to interest several shooting friends in my newly discovered method, however, one asked me to call back during halftime, and another told me that I have way too much time on my hands. It's like showing pictures of your grandchildren to strangers—is anyone really interested?

Sometimes, the cure for a too-ragged pattern is more shot out the end of the barrel. Within reason, heavier loads are a sensible solution, but it's easy to go too far. Overloads create another whole set of problems, this time behind the gun rather than in front of it.

If your patterns are still substandard, the gun itself can be improved. Older guns often have a steep shoulder at the chamber's forcing cone that adds to the upsetting forces in the shot stream. Back in the days of paper shells and fiber wads, the shoulder was necessary to prevent burning powder from blowing by the old-style wads. Modern plastic "skirted" wads seal well, making steep forcing cones obsolete. Without a lot of trouble or money, a gunsmith can elongate the forcing cone, and your patterns will improve remarkably. Similarly, the chokes themselves can be opened up through lapping or reaming, almost always resulting in less disruption to the pattern. Both are relatively inexpensive fixes.

If you want to go further, back-boring works miracles with patterns. The process increases the bore of the barrel by a couple thousandths and, for reasons that elude physical explanation, produces remarkable results. Years ago, when screw-in chokes were first being introduced, I sent my duck gun to a gunsmith in Seattle named Stan Baker. He back-bored the barrel and installed screw-in chokes. When I used plain-vanilla number 5s in that souped-up barrel with the .025 choke, the gun would routinely deliver 90 percent of the pellets evenly into a 30-inch circle at 40 yards. It was an amazingly deadly combination, and I killed a lot of ducks with that gun. But then the steel shot requirement came along a couple years later and changed everything. The ducks may laugh at me now, but for a while the mallard population trembled at the mention of my name.

As an aside about the business of patterning, I offer this anecdote: My friend and sometime shooting partner Chris Gulgin bought a new/old 16-gauge double to use as a grouse gun a while back. The choke in the barrels measured .003 and .010, equating to skeet and light-modified. That combination promised to be near ideal for the sort of woodland shooting he does in New England. But when Chris tested the double at grouse-shooting range, the barrels produced identical patterns. When he told me the story, he indicated the size of the patterns with a wide spread of his open hands: skeet and skeet.

He rechecked the choke dimension and did some additional pattern-ing, but the results were always the same—the gun threw identical patterns out of each barrel. On a lark, he tried a different brand of ammunition—same load and velocity, same shot size, same every-thing—just a different brand name. This time, the 25-yard results were what the chokes indicated they should be: his hands indicated a 30-inch skeet circle and a 24-inch light-modified second barrel. (With-out mentioning brand names, I can tell you that the first shells were dark green, and the more responsive ammunition was pale violet.) So remember the Chris Gulgin story whenever you run out of shells and stop in somewhere to buy more. I have proved to myself that velocity influences pattern quality, but here's evidence that perform-ance varies with brand as well.

When you produce a pattern sheet, those pellet holes are the result of a three-dimensional pattern striking a flat surface. In flight, the shot charge forms into a cloudlike swarm, but all you have left to examine is the two-dimensional result on a piece of paper. The ideal three-dimensional swarm is in the shape of a basketball, with the hindmost pellets not very far behind the leaders.

All the pellets inside a shotgun shell theoretically receive the same amount of energy and leave the barrel at the same speed. But in reality, part of the load loses some of its initial energy through fric-tion with the inside of the barrel or by deforming against other pel-lets. Those losses mean that some pellets travel through the air at slower speeds. When that happens, the in-flight swarm becomes elongated. Since the naked eye can't see a shot string in flight, few shooters ever consider it, but in the worst cases, the shot swarm can resemble a 30-foot-long cigar. Coarse shot, high velocity, overload-ing, small bores, soft shot, steep forcing cones, and tight chokes all contribute to internal friction losses and thus to the phenomenon of shot stringing.

Admittedly, all the pellets are moving a lot faster than the target, but it is conceivable that, with a little luck, a crossing target could pass right through such a strung-out pattern without being hit. A more likely result of shot stringing is that the target experiences a stretched-out series of little hits rather than the synergistic *ka-whump* when all the pellets arrive together. This is not a big deal when the target is clay, but a crippled bird can be the result in hunting situations.

Arguments rage on, with some pundits maintaining that the stringing effect is useful. I remain unconvinced. The proof is in the results: hard-hit gamebirds are dead on arrival, and those hit with strung-out patterns aren't—it's as simple as that. For best results in the field, stick with good-quality ammunition in reasonable loads to minimize the stringing effect.

Going hand in hand with the idea of the slot is the ability to estimate ranges when you're hunting. Just how far away is 35 yards? If a bird came out of that weed patch, would it be in range or just beyond? It's a skill that takes just a little practice. Golfers get pretty good at estimating yardage, and they're dealing with considerably greater distances that you are in shotgunning. The faces of the houses on a skeet field are exactly 40 yards apart; so are the utility poles on most residential streets. As you're walking around, get into the habit of estimating distances and then pacing them off. Once you get good at it, you'll see the results in the field.

GUN-LOAD-CHOKE COMBINATION

Some guns shoot better and some loads hit harder than others. If you accept that premise, it follows that there must be one best gun-load-choke combination that kills more cleanly and more often than any other. It varies with the game you're after, but each hunting situation has exactly one right combination.

When I speak of such an ideal combination, I don't mean to imply that you can't kill a bird with something else. Of course you can. People who know nothing about patterns and slots go hunting with lesser guns and inferior ammunition and still routinely bring birds home. But like the fellow who climbed the Himalayas barefoot, all that proves is that it *can* be done—not that it's the best way to go about it. The search for that one right combination is a search for consistency.

Ducks taken on the pass and the same ducks over decoys are different situations and require different gun-load-choke combinations. The one right gun for quail shooting might not be right for cornfield pheasants or for crossing doves. Stocked pheasants usually

Even the same bird at 30 yards can present 3 entirely different shots.

hold, while wild pheasants run, so the right pheasant load for one situation might not be right for the other. For that matter, the right combination often changes with the season and the weather. For example, early-season grouse, when there are leaves on the trees, need a different solution from grouse in November, when the leaves are down.

Years ago, the Polychoke company sold a lot of adjustable devices by targeting its ads to just such situations. And the argument still holds. Modern shotguns have provided a bit of latitude—you can screw in a different choke for a different situation and sometimes even install a different barrel. You don't have to change guns to know that your next shot is going to be effective. We tend to seek do-it-all solutions—a sort of skeleton key that will work in every lock. But like anything else heralded as "all-purpose," such universal combinations always involve a degree of compromise and are never exactly right for every situation. Confidence is all about knowing you're got the one right tool for the job at hand.

If you hunt only pheasants on a preserve with a flushing spaniel, or only woodcock in October with a pointing dog, or only sea ducks on the pass from the end of a jetty, you might be able to find one right combination and stick with it. But for the rest of us, who might conceivably do all of the above in the same day, we need to continually reassess the situation and be prepared to make changes.

When you put the decoys away and try your hand at high passing ducks, or when you finally get a chance to try for wild pheasants, or when the leaves are down and the distances in the grouse woods increase, the right gun-load-choke combination might be different than what you used earlier. If your results are going to continue to be consistent, you need to do your homework again. Chokes might need to be tightened, loads changed, and you might even find you need more gun—or less. Each situation has one right gun-load-choke combination. Find it, and consistency follows. The more you know about your shotgun, its chokes, and how it handles different loads and shot sizes, the more likely it is that you'll know the one best answer to a hunting situation and have it in your hands when the bird flushes. It's a good feeling.

You don't need to be a dreamer to expect consistent results when you've made a good shot. Clean kills are what you're after. Shock effect and reliable patterns deliver them consistently. Be flexible and learn to adjust to changing situations. It's one more step along the path to becoming a good shot.

Choke and Ammunition

Has modern ammunition made choke obsolete? Uncle Ralph's old shotgun might have been choked modified—at least, that's what was stamped on the barrel. The barrel miked-out at 16 thousandths of constriction. Fifty years ago, using that gun, he regularly shot pheasants at 40 yards with ordinary field loads of number 6 shot. Patterns at 40 yards showed that 60 percent of his load ended up inside a 30-inch circle—standard performance for a modified choke. Today, with the same gun and the same 1⅛ ounces of number 6 shot, the percentage of pellets inside the 30-inch circle might be 70 or even 75 percent—equivalent to "full" or "extra full" choke. Has the choke in Uncle Ralph's gun somehow tightened with age? Of course not. It's modern ammunition that has made the difference. Today's efficient loads put a lot more pellets where they're supposed to go. The *size* of the effective killing circle of the old gun is still the same; it's the *number of pellets* inside the circle that's different. So in truth, choke isn't obsolete, but the means of measuring it is.

CHOKE
The function of a shotgun's choke is to confine the randomness of individual hits to a specific area. Degrees of choke used to be expressed in terms of the percentage of pellets that hit within a 30-inch circle at 40 yards. That system was devised about 200 years ago during the muzzle-loader era, and modern gun writers continue the annoying practice of referring to choke by that long obsolete definition. Until recently, shotguns produced a lot of deformed pellets

that ended up somewhere other than in the pattern. But *scattergun* is no longer a descriptive term. With today's efficient ammunition, an up-to-date definition of choke would address the range at which a 30-inch circle of shot was produced.

As a rule of thumb, you might expect straight cylinder—that is, no choke at all—to throw a 30-inch circle of shot at 20 yards.* Skeet choke, with the very slightest constriction, throws a 30-inch circle at 23 yards. Improved cylinder is thought of as a 30-yard choke, modified is designed to produce a 30-inch circle at 40 yards, and full choke is meant for 50-yard work. There are steps in between modified and full, which is where "improved modified" falls; another step between improved cylinder and modified is "skeet-two," also known as "light-modified."

In reality, one company's "modified choke" might measure .705, while another company's "full" might have exactly the same constriction. There is no hard-and-fast standard. Likewise, you wouldn't assume a size "large" jacket would fit you without trying it on. The only logic the jacket's manufacturer used in deciding to label it "large" was that it's bigger than "medium" and smaller than "extra large." Similarly, choke names are relative—you've got to "try it on" to arrive at a useful and workable conclusion.**

Since the actual bore size of shotguns of the same gauge varies (especially in 12-gauge guns), simply measuring the outlet internal diameter of a barrel seldom tells the whole choke story. The pattern size and quality a barrel produces are best measured by the patterning experiment discussed in chapter 5. There are myriad factors that conspire to produce variations in expected choke performance—everything from shot size to muzzle velocity to the brand of ammunition used.

---

* About pattern size, please take note of an often misunderstood fact: skeet chokes are designed to throw a 30-inch circle at 23 yards, no matter what the gun's gauge might be. The same applies to improved cylinder, modified, and full—the size of the pattern is the same, regardless of the gauge. Bigger guns put out more shot and produce denser patterns, but similar chokes are supposed to produce similar-sized circles.

** There was a time when the screw-in choke companies tried to get away from names and just labeled their chokes with the amount of constriction, such as .005 or .020. Evidently, shooters weren't ready for that logical step, and the practice has been largely discontinued.

My first shotgun was a 20-gauge pump with a "modified" choke. It produced very nice patterns as long as I didn't use anything larger than number 8s. Patterns with number 7½ shot were ragged and full of bird-sized holes, and those with number 6 shot were nonexistent. I later bought a second barrel for the same gun that was marked "improved cylinder" and got years of upland service out of it, but I never figured out the mystery of the "modified" barrel. Ultimately, I used a hacksaw and converted it to a straight cylinder barrel for use in woodcock shooting.

Today, there are various types of "scatter" loads that prey on the obsolete percentage system of choke measurement, promising to "open up" a choke by scattering the shot charge in some manner. They don't work. That conclusion is obvious if you take the time to examine the results at a patterning board. You'll find that the pattern isn't spread at all; rather, it's ruined. Spreaders dramatically upset the flight of the shot string, and the result is a blown pattern full of big gaps. The amazing thing about the open-your-pattern gimmicks— spreader wads and sleeveless loads and square shot—is that some people actually buy them more than once.

When the need arises for maximum pattern spread, a hunter with an adjustable choke should go with straight cylinder combined with the slowest loads available and be happy with the results. Spreader loads may have some use when a gun is choked full and close shooting is necessary, but in that situation I'd borrow another gun before resorting to spreaders. Any bird hunter wants a better pattern, or maybe a larger one, but never less of a pattern, which is what you get when you drop a scatter load into the chamber.

AMMUNITION

Dr. Charles C. Norris wrote in 1946, "Indeed, present day cartridges are so excellent that it is difficult to imagine great future improvements."* He went on to celebrate the then-recent modernization of the folded crimp. The excellent shotgun shells of 1946 came in paper cases with fiber wadding. They contained "chilled shot," which, at the time, was a recent innovation made not from pure lead but from lead alloyed with a bit of antimony to make it harder. The shells also

---

* Charles C. Norris, *Eastern Upland Shooting* (J. B. Lippincott, 1946).

contained new types of gunpowder that permitted variations in shot charge and muzzle velocity—something relatively new in 1946. Old-style primers were made with mercury and were highly corrosive. Shells from Norris's time advertised "clean-bore priming," which, by inference, indicated that others were not so clean.

Things change, but something common to both 1946 and today is that pulling the trigger causes a bunch of lead pellets to instantly go from a standstill to 900 miles per hour. That's not acceleration—that's shock. Under such conditions, the little lead balls can get squeezed out of shape. Keeping them round is the one great and overriding challenge of all shot-shell efficiency.

There is a physical principle that says that round pellets fly true, but any that are even slightly misshapen won't end up where they're supposed to. All the improvements in shotgun ammunition, both before Norris's time and since, have amounted to better ways of keeping those pellets perfectly round. (The one possible exception was the introduction of the plastic hull. Plastic made repeating shotguns reliable.)

Shot protectors (usually an integral part of the plastic wad) keep the pellets from rubbing against the inside of the barrel and flattening out. In addition, it seems logical (although no one has ever proved it) that the shot protector imparts the constricting forces of the choke more evenly to the moving shot column.

Fiber wads permitted gas to blow by in the instant the shot charge passed between the open end of the shell and the start of the barrel's bore. Today's plastic wads are advertised as cushioning the shot column (which they do slightly) and reducing recoil (which they don't do at all). But the most unsung attribute of modern plastic wads is the sealing effect produced by the bottom skirt. Gas blow-by is nearly eliminated, and the full power of the shell goes into propelling the shot column forward. Shells are far more consistent from load to load than they were in the days of fiber wads, and the credit goes to the gas seal.

Among the things I learned while fooling around with patterns is that shot filler actually does what it claims to. (By filler, I mean the powdered or sometimes granulated plastic used to fill in the spaces between shot pellets during reloading. When it was first introduced,

Winchester called it "grix," and a lot of reloaders still use that name.) As explained to me, the stuff fills in the spaces in the shot column and cushions the pellets against crushing one another during their trip out of the shell and down the barrel. I've found that the larger the shot size, the better it works. Identical loads of number 6 pattern 20 percent better with grix filler than without, and number 4s show a 33 percent improvement. The stuff is amazing. Even number 7½ shot shows an improvement in the 10 percent range.

Unarguably, filler is a pain in the neck to work with—a shell must be removed from the reloading press after the shot has been dropped. A measured amount of the stuff is put into the loaded-but-not-crimped shell, then it's vibrated until the grix filler settles in among the shot. The process is best done in batches; I usually do 50 at a time. But if you're using coarse shot—that is, number 6 or better—you should be using buffered loads. They really work.

The highest-quality lead shot (labeled "magnum," "premium," or "high-antimony"—or sometimes all three) patterns better than ordinary lead shot (usually labeled "chilled"). The good stuff is "polished" so that the pellets start out round; the polishing process removes dimpled and deformed pellets from the mix. There is supposed to be sufficient antimony alloyed to harden the lead so that the round pellets stand a good chance of staying round. But because antimony is much more expensive than lead, manufacturers are stingy with it, and not all "magnum" shot is equally hard.*

Although it's believed to be a superior product, I've never found that copper-plated shot results in improved patterns. Nash Buckingham swore by it, but that was in the 1950s. Maybe a thick plating of copper was used back then that actually kept the pellets round, but today's "copper-plated" shot is little more than copper colored. It's

---

* Since antimony is not as heavy as lead, hard pellets are slightly lighter than soft pellets. Some argue that, because of this difference, soft pellets hit harder than premium shot does. The difference is mostly theoretical. In truth, you would need the services of a science lab to discern the minuscule weight difference between chilled and magnum shot pellets—it's less than 1 percent. In contrast, you need only a sheet of paper to see the difference in patterns. Hard shot produces patterns that are noticeably improved—as much as 10 percent better. In the clean-kill equation, pattern is the alpha factor that overshadows everything else.

expensive and looks pretty, but I suspect that it's just ordinary lead shot with a very thin coating of copper washed onto its surface—not thick enough to matter when push comes to shove, as it does immediately after the trigger is pulled.

However, European nickel-plated shot is thickly coated. It's hard and perfectly round, and it patterns and penetrates beautifully. Unfortunately, it's also very expensive.

We're all used to advertisements claiming that a product is "new" and "improved," and we tend to discount such claims. Today's premium-quality ammunition is the real McCoy. However, you can still buy junk ammunition that's no better than the stuff available 60 years ago. Every manufacturer produces a low-end economy load that is usually so cheaply made that even reloaders don't want the empties. You can be sure that such ammunition is made from the cheapest possible ingredients and that such a formula will never translate to consistent or efficient performance.

The argument for high velocity is not nearly as dramatic as some folks claim, yet people continue to pound themselves silly with high-brass loads year after year, believing that they're giving themselves an advantage. These are the same people who put high-octane gas in a Ford Escort. These shooters want the additional 130 feet per second that a high-velocity load offers (one fellow even had it figured out to an extra 89 miles per hour). The tripping point of their logic is that they're citing *muzzle* velocity—that is, the speed as the shot leaves the gun barrel. An unfortunate ballistic truth in shotgunning is that the faster a load starts, the faster it slows down. The finer the shot, the more pronounced the slowdown effect (30 yards downrange, the starting difference of 89 miles per hour in a load of number 7½s has dropped to 35 miles per hour). Coarse shot holds its velocity fairly well, but we don't use a lot of coarse lead shot in bird hunting anymore. You might make an argument for shooting pheasants with high-velocity number 6s, although the tables on pellet energy won't back you up.

When you hit a crossing pheasant at 40 yards, it matters greatly whether you hit it with just a couple of pellets—a hit that the bird will most likely survive—or with four or five pellets, which will almost certainly kill the bird outright from shock alone. That number of hits is a function of the shotgun's pattern. What does *not* matter in the "dead pheasant equation" is whether those pellets are traveling 491 miles per hour when they strike the bird (which is the speed of a standard load of number 6s at 40 yards) or going 31 miles per hour faster (the extent of the difference a high-velocity load would offer). Sufficient pellet hits are decisive, but extra velocity rarely amounts to anything positive. Some things bear repeating: the quality of the pattern matters on every shot, both near and far.

High velocity has recently become a selling point for otherwise ordinary ammunition: 12-gauge ⅞-ounce shells claim to be super high velocity, as if that somehow makes them better. Advertisers are hyping the high-velocity concept because light shot charges need that extra kick to guarantee that an autoloader (or a single-trigger double) will cycle. The unspoken part of the equation is that if you want soft-shooting light loads, you've usually got to load them yourself.

People talk about a gun "reaching out there." Somehow, high-velocity ammunition in the chamber and long barrels on a shotgun make people think that the range of the gun is extended. Nobody ever said that shot pellets couldn't fly that far. (I have a scar on my neck that proves number 4 shot can break the skin at 100 yards.) The trick is to get the pellets to fly that far and still be consistently effective. The one and only measure of shotgun effectiveness is consistency.

If it's a longer range you want, it doesn't come easy. Let's say you've been killing pheasants cleanly with a 1⅛-ounce load of number 6s in the 35- to 40-yard range with your modified-choked 12-gauge. That was me. Now, for some reason, you decide that you'd like to move out to 50-yard shots. That's me again, this time shooting driven pheasants out of milo stubble in the Texas panhandle.

Here's the thought process I went through:

• Patterns thin with range, so you've got to tighten your choke.

• Shot loses its velocity with range, so to keep the same shocking power, you've got to move up at least one shot size.

• But, when you do that, you've put fewer pellets in the same load, so you've got to either increase the amount of shot (by a lot) or tighten your choke some more—or both.

In my case, when I wanted 40-yard results at 50 yards, I had to move up to magnum 5s and choke down to full. I did, and I killed a few pheasants on that Texas hunt. But if you decide to do the same, you'd better do some long-range target practice, too. If, on a difficulty scale of 1 (easiest) to 10 (hardest), hitting a crossing shot with a modified choke at 40 yards is a 4, then hitting the same shot with a full-choked gun is a 6, and doing it at 50 yards is a 32.

The tables on pellet energy and downrange speed are about as interesting as some of the thermodynamic charts I used to read as a marine engineer: useful, but hardly recreational reading. Though dull, the statistics contain a few irrefutable truths. For instance, number 9 shot, no matter what its muzzle velocity, doesn't have enough pellet energy to do regular shock damage to a gamebird at 30 yards. It slows down too quickly to be a consistent game getter. Number 8 shot has half again the mass of 9s. That means two things: the larger pellet is heavier and thus has more shocking power, and the number 8 can retain its speed and shocking power over longer distances. Both 8s and 9s produce exemplary patterns, but the effective range of 8s is nearly 10 yards farther than that of 9s. No less an authority than Burton Spiller recommended 9s for grouse shooting, but that was in 1935. If he was alive today and could see the tables on ballistics, I believe he'd change his mind and recommend 8s, too.

Number 7½ shot evolved years ago to fill trap shooters' need for high-performance 8s—something to use on windy days or when the distance was stretched out an extra 2 or 3 yards. The 7½s are only slightly (17 percent) more massive than 8s, and the difference in pellet count is less than that. Although some writers insist on making a big deal of the difference between the two shot sizes, a hunter might use one or the other for an entire season and never suspect that a substitution had been made.

Also in the mix are the oddballs. Number 8½ shot produces wonderfully dense patterns and is ideal for first shots on flushing quail. And several of my friends use European number 7 shot in a nickel-plated version as a pheasant killer out of small-gauge guns.

Boxes of shotgun shells provide more printed information than most of us need: the gauge of the shells and their length, of course; the shot size; the weight of the load (1⅛ ounces, for example); and the relative strength of the powder charge, expressed in dram equivalents.* Recently, the expected muzzle velocity (in approximate terms) has been added. You'll also notice that the manufacturer lists recommended shot sizes for various gamebirds. For pheasants, 7½s, 6s, 5s, and 4s are recommended.

About that list of recommendations, I've found 7½s to be ideal. Consider, though, that I hunt pheasants with a pointing dog, so my first shot is usually at a range of 20 to 30 yards. Number 7½ produces superb patterns out of every gauge (except the .410) and carries enough shocking power to cleanly kill a rooster on the rise at skeet-field ranges.

When it comes to number 6s, I know a lot of people who use them for everything. My father was one such believer. Sixes pattern well—even out of the 20-gauge—and effectively hold their shocking power at long distances. In truth, a pheasant hunter routinely needs nothing larger. I like 6s in the tight barrel for any pheasant shot longer than skeet-field range.

I've used number 5s out of tight chokes on pheasants in the previously mentioned Texas panhandle hunts. In that situation, 5s killed crossing birds in a stiff prairie wind at remarkable ranges. I suspect that when tightly choked, 5s are effective at distances far greater than most of us can shoot accurately, myself included.

---

* At one time, the dram equivalent number was intended to translate the then-new innovation of smokeless powder into a format that could be understood by shooters accustomed to using black powder. Needless to say, the dram equivalent has outlived its purpose. The muzzle velocity number will soon supplant it.

But number 4s for pheasants? At normal ranges, 4s can be counted on to go right through any upland bird smaller than a turkey. Hit a bird with three pellets, and it'll have six holes in it. That's a bit of overkill. All that wallop gave number 4s the ability to penetrate goose down, which made them ideal for decoying geese and sea ducks. But since the nontoxic shot laws came along, number 4 lead shot no longer has a clear purpose. Some hunters still use 4s because of the false sense that something so powerful is deadly at long range. They forget how thin a pattern of coarse shot becomes beyond 40 yards. It is rumored that number 4 shot will soon be dropped by most ammunition makers.

For the past quarter century, duck and goose hunting has required nontoxic shot. For most of us, that has meant steel shot. In translating what we know about and expect from lead, there seems to be a general (albeit inexact) "steel shot equivalent" that holds up as long as you're not talking about long-range shooting: number 4 steel is similar in performance to number 6 lead, number 3 steel equates to number 5 lead, and number 2 steel substitutes for number 4 lead. Performance is about the same at close and medium ranges—something on the shy side of 40 yards—and the pellet count* in a 3-inch load of steel is close enough to be called the same as in a standard express load of lead shot.

Gun writers are prone to overstate the difference in effectiveness between steel and lead. One recent account likened it to the difference between Ping-Pong balls and golf balls, but that's a gross exaggeration. Steel shot patterns extremely well and is a proven performer, as long as you're talking about shots over decoys or anything

---

* Here are the actual figures: 1⅜ ounces of number 4 steel has 264 pellets, versus 281 pellets in a 1¼-ounce express load of number 6 lead. Number 3 steel's 217 is nearly the same as number 5 lead's 213, and number 2 steel's count of 172 is pretty much equal to number 4 lead's 169. None are exact matches, but close enough.

less than long ranges. But when ducks are buzzing by out beyond the rig (as they're prone to do on some days), steel's lack of long-range performance becomes evident. Such situations make water-fowlers wish they had coughed up the extra money for the new high-density lead-replacement shot. I've used it, and I can testify that the name-brand shot is every bit as effective as lead when the ranges are long. (I've opened up some off-brand shells and found that they contain clumped and misshapen pellets, which makes them very expensive junk.) The only problem I had with bismuth and tungsten matrix was the distraction of hearing the cash register ringing in the background each time I pulled the trigger.

Gauge and shot size are more closely related than most shooters suspect. Although all gauges handle fine shot fairly well, gauge is a limiting factor when coarse shot is used. Michael McIntosh explained the phenomenon better than I can.* As an example, he imagined a pair of 1-pound coffee cans—one filled with golf balls, the other filled with marbles. The marbles represent fine shot inside a loaded shotgun shell. They settle in and nest comfortably, minimizing the spaces between them. The golf balls correspond to coarse shot in a too-small gauge. They're just a little too big to fit comfortably and stack up at awkward angles inside the can. A taller can (equated to a 3-inch shell) doesn't help, because the can's inside diameter is the problem, and all a taller can will offer is space for more awkwardly positioned golf balls. When fired, the misaligned coarse shot pellets push against one another at strange and unpredictable angles and tend to scatter rather than fly true. The solution? Place the same number of golf balls in a 3-pound coffee can (equated to a larger-gauge gun), and suddenly they behave themselves and align as comfortably as the marbles did. When it is said that small gauges don't handle coarse shot very well, it is a function of this golf-balls-in-the-coffee-can phenomenon.

Every gauge has a limit beyond which the shot column is squeezed into a diameter that is too small to allow it to settle properly. The 20-gauge handles number 6 shot well, but nothing coarser. The 12-gauge seems to draw the line at number 4 shot. The 28-gauge

---

* See Michael McIntosh's essay in *The Grand Passage* (Countrysport Press, 1990).

doesn't handle number 6 shot very well. (I recently did some patterning with my shooting partner's 28 and found that number 7½ shot distributed itself predictably throughout a pattern, but number 6 shot produced spotty and ragged patterns at any range greater than 25 yards, regardless of which screw-in choke was employed.) That might help explain why a gun that is very efficient for quail might be found wanting when used with pheasant loads.

In view of the golf ball analogy, how large a gauge is needed to handle size BBB shot? How about size T? These shot sizes are routinely used in nontoxic goose loads these days. They amount to junior-varsity buckshot, and I don't know how big a gun would have to be to handle these loads properly. The patterns I see when I shoot that stuff out of my current 12-gauge duck gun are not encouraging.

As in all matters concerning shotguns, the measure of effectiveness is consistency. As I've pointed out elsewhere, you can be successful at just about anything using any gauge and load every once in a while. The real question is whether you can do so repeatedly. In selecting the best ammunition for the game you're after, the most important piece of information—the one that trumps everything else—will never appear on the flap of a box of ammunition: the effectiveness of the pattern, which translates into consistency, is something you've got to discover for yourself.

Wing Shooting Part 1:
Get Ready

In every clay target sport, the shooter takes time to get in the proper position: feet in the right place, shoulders and hips pointed correctly, hat adjusted. The gun is mounted, the tangled knot is obtained, and a few practice swing-throughs are made along the projected target line. Even when shooting low-gun (also known as international style), the shooter routinely does all that.* Only then is the gun butt lowered and the target called for, permitting the tangled knot to be quickly reestablished with a minimum of extraneous movement. The shooter can even get a preview of the target by saying, "Show me one." Supposedly clay target shooting is practice for hunting, but it's quite a stretch to equate the clay target "grooving-in" process to a bird hunter reacting to a sudden whir of wings from a weedy corner or an alder run. The shooting part is similar; it's getting to the shooting that's the rub.

As a hunter, you know that if you could somehow determine in advance what's about to happen, you could do what the clay target shooter does and align yourself properly for the upcoming opportunity. I have good news: you can. I'm not advocating carrying a cement pad around with you or training your dog to jump in and flush the bird when you yell "pull." However, you can do a few

---

* In the shotgun sport of FITASC, the shooter is not permitted to shoulder the gun at any time before the target is called for. That means no practice swing-throughs.

logical things to prepare for the shot and thus bring the skills you developed on the skeet field to bird hunting situations—that's the promise of this book, after all. The "get ready" list is a short one, and the topics are all interrelated:

- Become aware of the position of your shooting quadrant.
- Carry your gun effectively.
- Learn when and how to concentrate.
- Maximize your vision.

SHOOTING QUADRANT

One of the various limitations of our bodies is that right-handed people can't shoot to the right, and vice versa for southpaws. That is, most right-handers can shoot comfortably only through about 90 degrees of arc off to the left. If you were standing in the center of an imaginary clock face with your nose pointed at 12, that 90-degree arc would be from 9:00 to 12:00. To shoot farther to the right or left, you'd have to reposition your feet, and thus the clock face. So the

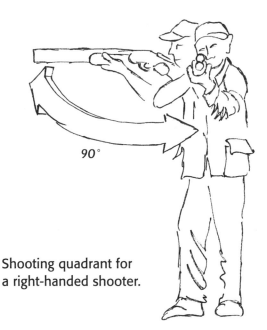

90°

Shooting quadrant for a right-handed shooter.

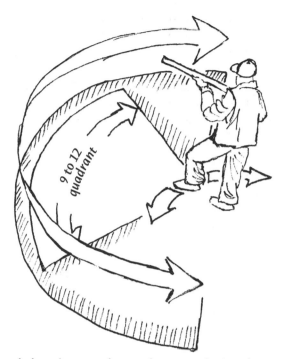

9 to 12 quadrant

Improved shooting quadrant when employing the one-step.

body's natural stops define and limit the 90-degree area you can shoot into. Let's call that your *shooting quadrant*.

I don't mean to suggest that right-handed shooters can't stretch and shoot to their right, ahead of the 12:00 stop, or to the left and rear, back beyond 9:00, because everyone does on occasion. But when we do, we don't hit much of anything because we can't keep the gun and our shooting eye in proper alignment—the tangled knot becomes untied beyond the body's natural stops.

The one-step was introduced in chapter 3. To review: if you are in a position to take a single step forward—not always feasible in tight quarters, and impossible while sitting—you can quickly reposition your shooting quadrant. Depending on where your left foot comes down at the end of the one-step, you can now make a shot into an expanded area of about 180 degrees—from 7:00 to 1:00.

But note that you still can't shoot to the right. Shooting into that area requires two steps and a full body turn. Even if you are quick on your feet and take just 1 second to execute the maneuver, a bird flying 30 miles per hour will have gone 15 yards farther by the time you begin to make your shot. No such repositioning movements are required if the shot comes up to your left. Therefore, right-handed hunters should strive to keep their left shoulders pointing in the direction they expect birds to appear.

Yet in the field, we all continue to place ourselves in situations where the limits of the human body work against us. Photos taken of hunters walking into a dog on point often become a case of what's wrong with this picture? The classic example is two right-handed bird hunters with guns at port arms as they walk into a dog's point. Sportsmanship dictates that birds on the left belong to the person on the left, and vice versa. You don't shoot across your partner's bow. Yet, because the fellow on the right is facing straight ahead, his shooting quadrant falls immediately in front of his partner. The only shot he's set up for is the one he's not supposed to take.

When quail hunting in Kansas, I'm often the one on the right, so you can paste me into that picture. For a long time, I mindlessly marched in facing straight ahead, even though I wasn't ready for the

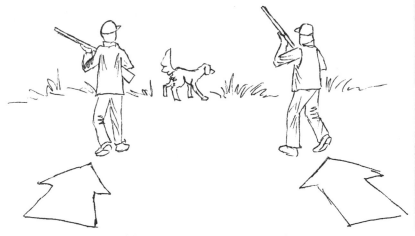

Quail hunters, mindless of quadrants.

counterclockwise

clockwise

shooting quadrant

shooting quadrant

A right and wrong path for a lone hunter over a dog's point.

shot I was hoping to get—birds in front of me or off to the right. I hope you're a faster learner than I was. It took a couple dozen covey flushes before I realized the handicap I was imposing on myself. Now, I approach the dog's point in a sidestepping motion, leading with my left shoulder, so that I'm prepared for shots on my own side. I'm not advocating that you walk around sideways all day like some giant land crab, but such adjustments make sense for the brief time you're walking in over a point and know ahead of time that you can't take shots to the left.

Similarly, when you're alone and approaching a point, on which side of the dog should you advance? If you go to the dog's left and the bird flushes from where the dog says it is, you're going to have to do some fancy footwork to swing your shooting quadrant around in time. Logic dictates that you set up for the scenario that's most likely. All things being equal, a right-handed shooter should always circle to the right in a counterclockwise approach.

Note the accompanying illustration of a fellow working a birdy strip. His dog is in the heavy cover, and he's on the edge. Maybe the wind is such that he's expecting the birds to cross in front of him once they flush, but barring that scenario, he's on the wrong side—any birds that flush will be on his right. No matter how good a shot he is at skeet, what he's doing is tantamount to facing the wrong

The wrong way to hunt a weed strip.

way on the shooting station. You wouldn't do that on the skeet field, so why put yourself at a disadvantage when hunting?

When waterfowling, it's no secret that you can't shoot much of anything while sitting in a canoe. I've hunted ducks out of various kinds of boats all my life, so I'm familiar with the limited range of motion inherent to sitting. You can fire your gun, but you can't shoot effectively—at least not through the sort of arc required by most shots. Whenever possible, I get out and stand in the water next to the boat. That way, I'm on my feet, with all the advantages that position imparts to my shooting.

Nevertheless, there will be times when, for one reason or another, you must shoot from a sitting or kneeling position. Maybe you're off-shore gunning for sea ducks (as I am in the accompanying photo), or perhaps you're in a layout blind in a cut cornfield or on a wide-open salt marsh. In that case, be as fussy as you have to be. Arrange your shooting position ahead of time so that you put your effective 9:00-to-12:00 quadrant where the birds are expected to pass. Reposition your blind as needed; use a second anchor to make sure the boat maintains

Sea duck hunting.

the right angle to the decoys. Do whatever it takes to be loyal to your one best chance.

You already know that birds don't always appear where they should. Sometimes ducks come from behind you or they buck the wind and work in from the wrong side. When that happens, you're going to grit your teeth and say some words you wouldn't use in polite company. But you've only got one best place to position your quadrant, and that ought to be in the area with the greatest promise of success.

GUN-CARRYING POSITION

I have a pet theory that shooting success is directly proportional to the amount of time a hunter spends with both hands on the gun. Certainly, you can't take even a casual walk through an upland covert and keep your gun at the ready every moment—you need your hands for other things as well. But returning both hands to the gun means that you'll be ready when an unexpected opportunity arises.

Many years ago, I read an article by Tap Tapply on the time it takes to mount a gun from various carrying positions. I couldn't locate that article, so I did my own research with a shooting partner and a stopwatch. The carrying position that required the longest time to get the gun into action is the one seen so often in outdoor pictures. I call it the "rabbit hunter's carry," with the gun stock tucked into the crook of the arm and the muzzle pointing down-ward. It took 1.6 seconds to grab the shotgun, get it to my shoulder, and fire an accurate shot. A bird flying away at 30 miles per hour would travel 70 feet in that time. The next slowest was the "tired man's carry," with the gun held with one hand like the handle of a briefcase: 1.3 seconds. Things weren't much better when the gun was carried like a marching infantryman, with the hand on the butt plate and the receiver resting on the shoulder. It took 1.2 seconds to wrestle the gun into position and get off a shot.

It's significant that none of these three carrying positions had the shooting hand on the gun's grip. A big improvement came from positions that did. With the gun held across folded arms it took just 0.7 second to get a shot off. A similar time was turned in by starting with the gun's rib resting back on the shoulder, as you might carry it while using your left hand to fend off brush and branches.

Then there were the positions with both hands on the gun. From the "relaxed port arms" position, lifting the gun to the shoulder and firing an accurate shot took 0.6 second. The "high port" carry shaved a tenth of a second off that time. And, as you might suspect, fastest of all—at 0.4 second—was "low gun," with the forward hand extended.

The rabbit hunter's carry.

The briefcase carry.

The infantryman's carry.

Two faster carrying positions.

The three fastest carrying positions.

That's the "get-ready-to-shoot" stance that most of us use at sporting clays or when we're walking in over a point. The same bird that got 70 feet away with the "rabbit hunter's carry" would manage to fly only 18 feet from its takeoff point if you were in the "low gun" position when you made the flush.

This book is intended to help you translate your clay target shooting skills to hunting situations, and here's another step toward that goal. With both hands on the gun—particularly with your trigger hand on the grip and your finger on the safety button—you don't have to take the extra time to find it when the moment arrives. The preceding experiment shows that if you're at least close to being ready when an unexpected bird flushes, you have a better chance of success. Admittedly, you can't walk around with a shotgun in the "get ready" position all day long. There are logical times during any day afield when you can relax and know that your gun won't be needed in the immediate future. But all hunting involves being prepared, and keeping both hands on the gun is the best way to do that.

About the business of carrying a loaded shotgun, here's an aside: Straight-grip stocks—sometimes called English-style stocks—are all the rage these days. They look racy and are often featured on lightweight field guns. Although the gun's weight is reduced by half an ounce or so by eliminating the pistol grip, the wrist must be twisted into an unnaturally convoluted position to carry such a gun. That's bad mechanics, and such hyperextension will lead to problems. I know, because I carried straight-grip guns for 12 years, and it's a medical miracle that I don't have ligament damage as a direct result. The ergonomic configuration of a pistol-grip stock permits the gun to be carried (and shot) with the wrist in a natural position.

Originally, the excuse for the straight-grip design was to permit the hand to be moved on the stock to work both triggers of a two-trigger gun, but I've shot two-trigger guns most of my life and never needed to move my hand. It's difficult to imagine anyone with hands so small that they couldn't move the inch or so between the triggers on most guns. Consider, too, that the English gentry who favored the design had flunkies standing nearby to hand them their guns when the time came for shooting. The flunky might have suffered from ligament damage because of the straight stock, but not m'lord.

CONCENTRATION

I've become an evangelist when it comes to concentration. Lack of concentration is the reason why a clays shooter might drop the last of six targets after proving on the first five that he knew how to break them. Letting the attention wander is why a double-A skeet shooter sometimes misses low seven. Not concentrating at the right time is the most common mistake among those who already know how to shoot.

Think of a baseball player. He employs three different levels of concentration. There are times between innings and when he's on the bench and, although his attention is on the game, he can relax and look at the pretty girl in the stands behind third base. When he's in the field, he's at the next level of concentration; he's constantly thinking of the various things he must do if the ball is hit here or there. But his concentration is never more intense than when he's at the plate and the pitcher goes into his windup. Everything else—his swing, his stance, his expectations—should have been worked out beforehand, because his undivided attention must be on the flight of the ball.

There are times during a bird hunt when you might be the ball-player between innings. You can put the gun on your shoulder and enjoy the scenery, because you're crossing an unproductive area or walking a farm road with the dog at heel. But when you're actively hunting, you should adopt the mentality of the fielder between pitches. During an entire game, an infielder might see only two or three balls hit to him, but he's got to be ready on every pitch. Likewise, a hunter must continually anticipate what might happen in the next few yards. For every apple tree with a grouse in it or under it on an October afternoon, there are 999 other vacant trees. The only way you're ever going to be ready when Mr. Thunderbird announces his presence is to assume he's under the tree you're approaching, even though you'll be wrong most of the time. Consider what's likely and what's not, and figure out how you'll react if and when it happens. If there's a bird under that apple tree up ahead, which way will it probably go? What if it comes up before you get there? What if it waits until you're right on top of it? It's an ongoing process that requires rethinking and reassessment. If the bird runs, where will it go? If it's in that deadfall, which direction will it take once it's flushed? From which side can you get the better shot?

Gamebirds often behave predictably. Some—bobwhite quail are a prime example—can be relied on to fly toward the nearest heavy cover, even if you're standing in their way. Others, such as pheasants and doves, need open spaces, and their flight paths take them in that direction. Woodland grouse are reluctant to cross openings, but woodcock usually head for the brightest patch of sky. Decoying ducks, however else they might maneuver, predictably land into the breeze. When any bird flushes, it initially flies up into the wind, even if it immediately turns in another direction to escape. That fact alone—knowing where the bird is going at the instant of takeoff—might give you the extra fraction of a second that makes the difference between success and frustration. But you can't use any of that information to your advantage unless you're thinking about it ahead of time.

"As soon as you stop thinking, you invariably pay the price." That's a grouse shooter's axiom that I often repeat, usually to myself after I've allowed my attention to wander and was unprepared when a bird took flight. Most shots are conventional, and most birds flush in a predictable manner from a predictable place. If you're paying attention—that is, if you're concentrating—you should constantly be making those predictions and adjusting your position accordingly. The fellow on the wrong side of the birdy strip may have been thinking about what he was going to have for supper, but he certainly wasn't thinking about where he expected birds to flush. The guy who went to the left of his dog's point wasn't thinking about his shooting quadrant either. When the bird went out hard right, the shooter took so much time to get into position that the shot ended up being much longer than it needed to be. And what about me and my quail-hunting story with the same unhappy ending over and over? From my position on the right, the bulk of the covey often quartered away left-to-right in front of me, just as I had hoped they would. But I ended up rushing my shots every time because I continued to unthinkingly set up for a shot to the left—one that I wasn't supposed to take anyway.

Once the bird is in flight, making the shot requires the same total and undivided attention that a batter gives to a pitch delivered to the plate. Genuine concentration amounts to just 1.5 seconds' worth of blotting out everything but the task of hitting, whether the object is a bird or a baseball. In the next chapter, I address the various permutations of actually hitting birds that are trying hard not to be hit. Right now, it's enough to say that it *can* be done, as long as you've done the groundwork and prepared for this moment. The learned aspects of shotgun shooting need to be practiced until they become automatic reactions. Putting the safety off, "cheeking" the stock, finding the line of the bird—all that has to be part of your conditioned, unthinking response. If it's not, then your attention is divided, and your concentration is less than total.

The act of shooting a bird is brief and often arrives unannounced. Being ready at the right time is what the game is all about—even though those occasions might be hours and miles apart. It doesn't mean walking along on the edge of hysteria for the entire day; rather, it means being able to recognize the times and places where concentration is necessary and reacting accordingly.

VISION

Statistics rarely tell us anything new. Mostly, they verify things we already suspected. One example is distilled from my 35 years of gunning diaries: the better I see the bird, the better my shooting percentages. That's a universal truth—not just for me, but for all shooters. We hit the high ones better than the low ones because we see them better. It's the reason why we do better on 8:00 ducks than on the early ones that show up at first light. It's also the reason why everyone's grouse-shooting percentages go up once the leaves are down—the leafy branches that earlier screened the birds' flight are now bare. It's safe to say that regardless of range or flight angle, we all shoot our best when the bird is clearly seen.

As a caveat, I might add that a clearly seen bird in its natural environment is not a routine occurrence. Sometimes we can see the bird, but not clearly—it's in the shadows or playing the grayish-bird-against-a-grayish-background trick. Shooting averages come down a notch in those situations. When the bird is just a glimpsed blur as it darts away, shooting expectations are poorer still. Worst of all are the situations when the bird becomes obscured just as the shot is made—it either flies behind some screening foliage or is swallowed by a dark shadow and remains hittable but unseen. In all those situations, the automatic reaction is to lift your head to see better. That rarely has positive results. After those uncertain shots, the thump of a bird hitting the ground is sometimes heard, but that happens far more often in outdoor stories than in real life.

Once the bird is in flight, it's too late to do anything about your vision or the lighting, but there are a few things you can do to prepare for less-than-optimal conditions. People who are familiar with cameras know that the wider the lens is open, the more difficult it is to put things in proper focus. That same phenomenon is at work in the lens of your eyes—the darker it is, the wider your eyes open, and the more difficult it is to focus on anything moving. So it stands to reason that you should adopt hunting habits that maximize the amount of light reaching your eyes. But too often, the tendency is to do things that work in the opposite direction.

In terms of our vision, the outdoor world is divided into two halves—everything above the horizon is bright, and things on the ground are relatively darker. Our pupils automatically dilate or contract when our vision moves from bright to dark areas or vice versa, but it takes a moment. Because of that phenomenon, looking down as you walk in to flush a bird is always a mistake. Certainly, you need to see where you're going, but you can accomplish that with your peripheral vision. I'm addressing here the counterproductive practice of searching for the bird on the ground.

You rarely satisfy your curiosity and see the bird before it flushes, but that's not why the habit is a bad one. The problem is related to the way your eyes adjust to the relative darkness of the weeds and tangles at your feet. When the bird springs up, it immediately passes into the brightness of the upper half of your vision, and it takes a moment for your eyes to react. A duck hunter in a blind, keeping his face down as the ducks work the rig, is at a disadvantage when he looks up into the relative brightness of the dawn sky. A worst-case scenario finds a guide keeping everyone concealed until he springs a trap door and everyone who had been in the darkness is suddenly expected to find a target in the bright sky. Depending on how young your eyes are, that moment can be brief (for young whippersnappers), or it can take a second or two (for the rest of us). However long it takes, it's too long. When walking in to flush a bird, a much more productive practice is to shift your focus to some object above the horizon. That way, when the bird appears against the sky, your eyes have already adjusted.

Another consideration is your hat. Is it working for or against your shooting? I'm not a big fan of baseball caps, at least not for shotgun shooting. With my long face, I have a tendency to incline my head forward when I lean into the stock as I mount the gun. The long visor of the cap sometimes cuts into my vision, and I automatically lift my head to see better. I've seen fellows do the same thing when wearing cowboy hats. At best, a hat brim cuts down on the amount of light reaching your eyes. Couple that with the fact that the act of mounting a shotgun cuts off the lower half of a shooter's vision, and suddenly the amount of available light has been considerably reduced just at the moment you need it the most. That's hardly a problem on bright, sunny days, when there's more than enough light to go around. But when it's gloomy or the light is otherwise less than optimal, a short-brimmed hat makes a lot more sense.

Then there's the question of your shooting glasses. Shooting glasses are supposed to help you see things better, but that's not always the case. As with so many other aspects of shotgunning, we try to seek a one size-fits-all solution to a complex problem. We want to put on one pair of glasses and have them be right for all conditions. But outdoor light varies, and the right glasses on a gloomy, overcast day might work against you in a different set of conditions—even later in the same day. Ideally, the amount of tint in your shooting glasses should be just enough to keep you from squinting. Anything darker will prevent the optimal amount of light from reaching your eyes, thus impairing your ability to focus.

Clay target shooters have come up with countless variations of color and darkness to help fluorescent-red targets stand out against various backgrounds, but in the field, you're usually trying to focus on a blurred bird against a grayish background, and for that, you need all the light you can get. The universally popular yellow lenses *seem* to make things brighter by increasing contrast (they make the darks darker), but they do that at the expense of filtering out a large portion of the available light—as much as 50 percent. In field shooting, maximizing light trumps all other considerations. So if you're not squinting, you probably don't need any tint at all in your shooting glasses.

Do you have shooting glasses in your distance prescription? Here's some unsettling news: human eyesight starts degrading at 11 years of age. If you're older than 11, your depth perception, strength of focus, and ability to sort things out in less-than-optimal lighting were all slightly better last year than they are now. If you're wearing glasses to read this, chances are it's not just your close vision that is impaired; your distance vision can probably be improved on, too. My quail-shooting partner significantly improved his percentages when he finally bought distance-vision lenses for his shooting glasses (then he wondered why he waited so long). If your shooting is important to you, invest in a pair of prescription shooting glasses.

That's the end of the "get ready" list: four very important things to work on before the bird takes flight. If you know any good shots, it's a safe prediction that they are aware of their shooting quadrant (even if they call it by a different name) and that they lead with the left shoulder when expecting a shot. They seldom carry a shotgun without having both hands in the shooting position. There aren't many birds that take them by surprise because they don't indulge in a lot of daydreaming while hunting. These good shots may be sharp-eyed old-timers, but if they wear glasses, it's a safe bet that they've given them some thought as well.

As any hunter knows, sometimes *the bird happens to you*. That's luck. But when *you happen to the bird*, that's successful hunting. Some hunters who are good shots seem to be lucky, but mostly they create their own luck by doing their homework. Getting ready is about thinking logically and then acting on the conclusions you reach. What happens once the bird is in the air is the subject of the next chapter.

Wing Shooting Part 2:
Shoot Flying

The highest point on Cape Cod is called Shoot-Flying Hill. For me, that name has always conjured up images of what must have been going on back when places were being named: men with flintlocks taking pass shots as ducks traded from one side of the Cape to the other, or maybe old-time market hunters with live decoys trying to entice migrating geese to stop at the hilltop. Wherever the name came from, it's an appropriate title for a chapter on wing shooting.

Back in chapter 1, I made the statement that gamebirds are easy to hit. It's time to examine that statement further. For the sake of illustration, consider a longish crossing shot on a sporting clays course—35 yards or so. It's going to be the same target presented as a report pair. When it's your turn, you call for the target, swing the gun along the flight path, and keep the muzzle moving, but you miss. You try to move the gun faster on the second target, but you miss again. On the next pair, you take the target a bit sooner and get two clean breaks. Once you've got it right, the third pair is duck soup, and you leave the station having broken four of six. Not bad.

Now let's persuade a series of rooster pheasants to fly the same path as the 35-yard crossing target. Pheasants are bigger and more easily seen than an edge-on clay target, and they'll be making a commotion as they pass. It's not a stretch to say that you'd do as well on the pheasants as you did on the clays. You might even do even better than four for six, since you'd probably take a second shot at any pheasant you missed with the first one. Of course, in the field, you won't see six identical shots in the space of 3 minutes, so you can't make adjustments as you go—you've got to get it right the first time. But the point is that a crossing 35-yard pheasant isn't a very difficult chance.

In the "easy-to-hit" equation, you can substitute any opportunity on any gamebird that you routinely see in the field. If you bring the same speed and angle to a skeet range or sporting clays course, you would likely do pretty well. The point is that, in bird hunting, the shots themselves are not inherently difficult. Of course, there are unmakeable shots, but these are seldom the result of anything spectacular the bird does while in flight—gamebirds don't routinely perform aerial acrobatics to avoid being hit, after all. Rather, the unmakeables are usually related to being in the wrong position at the time of the flush. When your natural shooting quadrant is lined up entirely wrong, shots become a hopeless waste of ammunition. Thus, birds that flush behind your right elbow are often in the unhittable category. Ditto for birds that jump on the left flank and angle to the rear.

The speed of any gamebird is a subjective thing, influenced by cover and distance. A ruffed grouse blasting out of a deadfall seems to be going a lot faster than its maximum of 30 miles per hour. The fact that it's all happening in close quarters and that the bird is going top speed right off the ground adds to the illusion of swiftness, as does the fact that you can hear the roar of the rocket engine when the bird takes flight. Consider, too, that bobwhite quail fly no faster as a covey than they do as singles, but the explosive extravaganza of a covey flush makes it seem like you're not quick enough. Yet singles— at the same speed—are relatively routine.

Pheasants on the rise are relatively slow targets, but when a rooster has a head of steam, he can sail along at 50 miles per hour. Hen pheasants seem to fly better than roosters, although neither are aerial acrobats. They don't do a lot of dipping and diving, but doves do. Unlike pheasants, doves seem to have several speeds in flight and can fly as fast (or as slow) as they need to in every situation.

When there are gunshots echoing behind them, doves can seemingly out-
fly their shadows.

We all miss shots while hunting, and not just the tough ones,
either. It's not a question of marksmanship—we prove that each time
we visit the skeet range. The purpose
of this book is to help you translate
your clay target shooting to hunting situations, so here, I've coupled
some common gamebird opportunities with a common shooting fault
committed in the field. No mistake is unique to any one gamebird—
we're all capable of making any number of shooting errors regardless of the type of feathers the target is wearing. See if you recognize
a few of your own.

GROUSE, HITTING THE CURVEBALL, AND FINDING THE SWEET SPOT IN TIME

When the subject is the ruffed grouse, remember that skeet was originally designed as practice for hunting that very bird. The relatively
close ranges and jackrabbit-quick target speeds of skeet replicate
those seen by grouse hunters in woodland coverts. A grouse hunter
sees multiple variations of every shot seen on the skeet field during
the course of a hunting season, albeit with a few trees thrown in.

The grouse is innately nervous, but good bird dogs can point
them. My best dog in her best year pointed 34 percent of the grouse
we encountered, but about 20 percent is the norm for most good bird
dogs. Even when pointed, it's a rare grouse that will hold tight until
the hunter kicks it out. As such, the quartering shots from low six
and high two represent the shots most often seen by grouse hunters.

Quartering chances give rise to the fable that grouse purposely
put trees between themselves and the hunter as soon as they flush.
The implication is that a bird with the IQ of a barnyard chicken not
only understands the workings of a firearm but also has figured out
how to negate its effectiveness. Not likely. The fact is, it's all but

Low-six as a grouse shot.

impossible for a bird *not* to fly behind a tree in the woods. Angularity determines that the spaces between the trees become smaller as the bird bends away. It's the venetian blind principle at work: you see the bird well, but by the time you get the shot off, you're firing at a wall of tree trunks. Unless taken quickly, quartering shots in the woods are exercises in frustration.

Grouse can, however, be credited with great maneuverability on the wing, and they dip and swerve around tree trunks and limbs as they depart. Even though we expect (and even practice for) straight-line flight paths, we often see otherwise—with all gamebirds, not just grouse. Ducks fly in a tight radius as they circle into the decoys, quail coveys flush in random directions and quickly bend to get back together, birds on the wing change their minds and bank left or right to follow a new direction.

Such curveball shots seem difficult. Finding the line isn't easy, because it's changing. But don't make the shot more difficult than it really is. You're not shooting dimes with a .22, after all. Your pattern is roughly 30 inches wide inside your effective slot, and you don't have to be dead center on the bird to make the shot. Using a short, compact swing negates the distracting effect of a curving flight path.

The compact swing is the natural result of combining the gun mount with moving the muzzle along the line of the target. The melding of these two functions can take place only after you've got the hang of each one separately. They have to be learned independently, but in practice, they are often combined until one is undistinguishable from the other—a necessity if shots are to be taken quickly. The compact swing is the answer to the curveballs thrown by grouse, as well as the quirky flight of woodcock and snipe, the compound down-curve of a decoying mallard, the curvilinear flight of a flushing quail, and the chondelle target in sporting clays.

A truism of wing shooting is that if you wait long enough, every shot will turn into a straightaway. Another school of thought says that there are only two types of shots: diminishing lead and increasing lead. All this makes for an interesting discussion, until you consider that the bird is within your 10-yard effective slot for only a second or two. Knowing when to shoot is as important as knowing how. Based on your abilities and reaction time, your brain recognizes the one right moment in the target's flight when everything comes together. That moment is called the sweet spot in time, and it isn't unique to grouse hunting. It applies to all forms of shotgunning. As long as you can identify the line of the bird, the computer part of your brain is able to "see" the sweet spot out there in front of the moving target. The sweet spot is out there for only an instant, and any hitch that causes you to miss it results in a hurry-up effort, even though the bird might still be in reasonable range. That may explain why so many second and third shots are fruitless. If the sweet spot slips away, you're usually better off saving your shotgun shells for the next time.

Whenever I devise illustrations for finding the line of the target, I always draw the line as a long, continuous vector. It makes for interesting pictures, but in field shooting—particularly fast and close grouse hunting—your brain doesn't need a long line. In all forms of bird shooting, the information you need from the line is not the big picture—where is the bird going?—but rather the small picture—where will it be an instant from now? In grouse shooting, sometimes all you get is a glimpse of the bird, but that may be all you need. You're interested only in enough of a line segment to swing the gun along.

Being able to take advantage of the sweet spot in time may be the difference between veteran bird hunters and a not-so-veteran: Beginners tend to rush, sure that they don't have enough time to catch up with the bird. Experienced hunters can't be slow, to be sure, but they don't succumb to the temptation to rush the shot. Certainly, the unexpected roar of wings can take any of us by surprise, and no bird hunter is always as methodical as he should be. But a shot-gunner who has acquired the necessary gun-handling skills will have attention left over to concentrate on hitting the bird. When that happens, the sweet spot in time becomes obvious.

Years ago, when Burton Spiller and William Harnden Foster wrote their grouse-shooting classics, they each described what they considered to be the most difficult chance. Both of them cited the same shot: a grouse that makes a power dive straight down out of a tree, then levels off just above the ground and flies away from the gunner. Both men wrote of bird shooting during the World War II era in the same northeastern coverts where I do my hunting. Evidently, things have changed. My grouse-hunting career started in 1964, and I've seen a grouse perform that maneuver a grand total of once. Treed grouse often flush straightaway, as in a high-one shot. Alternatively, where the cover is thick, they'll flush upward to reach flying room above the forest canopy, but power dives of the sort that Spiller and Foster wrote about are unknown, and I can't imagine why.

The most difficult grouse shot I routinely see is something I call the "up-and-down trick." The bird flushes in a standard low-seven manner, with a rising flight path, then abruptly changes its mind and heads for the deck. The result is a humpbacked line of flight that you just can't stay with: the bird turns downward just as you're pulling the trigger. It's the bird-shooting equivalent of the split-fingered fastball. The up-and-down trick isn't unique to the ruffed grouse. In brushy cover, I've seen bobwhites do their own version of the maneuver, and I'm told that chukars and ptarmigan (both of which fly very much like grouse, but in more open spaces) perform the same stunt, but I haven't hunted either bird enough to say for sure.

I don't have a good answer for hitting grouse when they do the up-and-down trick, since, as with the split-finger pitch, you never really expect it. When I've been successful, it's been with the second barrel. Sometimes you can wait them out, but in typical grouse cover, birds are often out of sight before they're out of range, so waiting is seldom a productive strategy.

About hunting in the woods: shooting through the inevitable screen of branches and brush can be productive—

The up-and-down trick.

on most grouse-shooting opportunities, it's either that or nothing—but the screen will eat up a portion of the effective pattern. By one estimate, 75 percent of the shot in any grouse load never reaches the ground. For that reason, *volume* of shot is the trump card in selecting grouse loads. Small-gauge guns with their small shot charges don't always produce acceptably consistent results in grouse coverts.

One of the observations I've made while following my bird dogs for the past 40 years is that there seems to be a statistical "law of threes" governing grouse shooting: if you flush three birds, there'll be one that you only hear, one that you see but have no chance to shoot at, and one that you have a chance at, but it's seldom an easy one. Therefore, you get to shoot at only one out of three, and if your shooting is anything like the rest of ours, you'll miss two-thirds of the time. Statistically, then, for each grouse taken, a hunter has to move nine. Apply that figure to the flush rate in a typical year (1.8 flushes per hour), and a hunter might expect to take one bird for every 5 hours of hunting. Then consider that a pair of grouse fillets weighs in at 10 ounces. If you pay yourself for your time (the working wage for a laborer these days is $12 an hour), without counting the cost of guns, ammunition, bird dogs, licenses, gas, and whatnot, grouse on the table goes for $80 per pound.

Unquestionably, there isn't enough "hunt" in grouse hunting to go out solely for the sake of the birds you might bring home—not at that price, anyway. I'm certain that every upland bird hunter and waterfowler could do similar calculations.

QUAIL, THE HINGE, AND IMPETUS

A long time ago, Havilah Babcock wrote that to be successful at quail shooting, you've got to get on the same train they want to ride. I scratched my head over that one for a while, but then I did some bobwhite hunting, and it quickly became clear: when flushed, a covey of bobwhites usually flies for the nearest cover (the same is true of scaled quail, locally known as blues in the Texas panhandle). In Babcock's terms, the train they want to get on is heading that way. You can either get aboard the train or get run over by it, but you're not likely to change its direction. Of course, you can try to steer a covey into the open or drive it in a more favorable direction, but if you're in the way, the covey is likely to flush right back over you. If you get any shooting at all, it'll be at birds whizzing by your hat brim. It's better to walk in from a direction that will push the covey where it wants to go anyway. In that case, quail shooting becomes one of several variations of just one shot: low-house seven.

Complicating what should be easy shooting is the explosive extravaganza of a dozen birds taking wing at the same time. Quail hunters always advise against the mistake of flock shooting. "Pick a bird," they say, as if it were a commandment. In that respect, I've rarely had any trouble. I get my comeuppance when the covey is scattered over an area the size of your living room and the birds get up like a string of Chinese firecrackers going off: one, then a pair, then another single, then three, then two more, than another one. Just as I'm pulling on a bird, another one gets up closer to me, and I switch to that one, and then to another. In the confusion, there have been occasions when the entire covey has departed and I've still got two full shells in the chambers.

Quail—or any other gamebird—are expected to rise as they take wing. In thick cover, they usually do, but in the open, bobwhites go with plan "low A." This involves the idea that the shortest distance between two points is a straight line, and the point they've got in mind is someplace out of gun range. They fly off just above the top of the weeds, meaning that the shot would be below eye level. The natural reaction to such below-the-horizon chances is to point the gun downward. But when you do that, the tangled knot tends to come untied. In chapter 3, I emphasized the importance of swiveling from the hips so that the gun mount stays locked up. It's equally important on below-

The hinge.

eye-level shots—you've got to imagine that you're hinged.

Don't make the mistake that the young man in the accompanying photo is making. It's obvious that his downward gun point has lifted his head off the gun stock, and he's not going to hit much of anything that way. The weirder the shot, the more important it becomes to stay locked up above the waist, and they don't get much weirder than below-eye-level chances.

Below-eye-level shots, the right way and the wrong way.

Good overhead form.

You seldom see the opposite extreme when hunting quail, but dove hunters, waterfowlers, and woodcock shooters sometimes get high-angle overhead shots. The same "hinged" thinking applies here as well, although it requires some footwork to lean back as far as necessary. In the photo, the gunner is showing the proper form for stepping back with the off foot, allowing you to shoot nearly straight upward and still keep the knot tightly tied.

When quail cooperate and flush as expected—that is, rise as they take wing—you might act as you do on the pad at low-seven: approximate the line, get the muzzles in front, and keep them moving after the shot—and then send the dog to make the fetch. Since the bird is rising, getting the muzzles in front means blotting the bird out so that it's not visible at the moment you pull the trigger. Misses occur when the shooter knows the shot is a tough one and peeks in order to keep the rising bird in sight and thus be ready for the second shot.

Sometimes you do everything right but still shoot "over the top." Why? There is an effect in the gun mount that I call *impetus*. To demonstrate how it can affect your shooting, think of using a 10-foot-long section of ½-inch galvanized pipe in place of a shotgun, which weighs about the same. Hold the pipe at port arms, with your right hand where the trigger would be and your left hand corresponding to its place on the fore end. Now, from that position, mount the "gun" and make believe you're shooting at a target. What happens? As you swing the pipe forward and down with your left hand to start the gun mount, the far end gets out of control and bounces on the ground in front of you. When you try to continue the mount and lift the pipe to your shoulder, the far end jumps upward, taking a strong effort to settle. There is some wavering of the "muzzle" as you fight to get it under control, but after some effort, you're pointing at the target. That's an example of impetus gone crazy.

It has to do with Newton's first law of motion: a body in motion tends to remain in motion. The motion you imparted to the end of the galvanized pipe remained in effect until it was countered by another force—in this case, the striking of the ground. There are exaggerated leverage forces at work in something as long as a 10-foot piece of pipe, and the forces of impetus aren't as great in a shotgun, but they're still there.

The act of mounting a shotgun often describes a path that has several angles. It all has to be done in sequence, and each change of angle requires a correction force to put the gun's movement on a new path. The longer the gun, the more it resembles the 10-foot piece of pipe. You can get away with this sort of thing when the gun is mounted slowly, but speed things up—as you're likely to do when the whir of wings announces that it's show time—and the precise forces and counterforces required won't match up in time and space. The result: the gun mount is sloppy, and the right path won't be traced in time for an accurate shot.

Don't believe it? Let's go back to the skeet field, where you're shooting low seven. Mount the gun, call for the bird, lift the muzzles slightly, and smash the target. When the gun is premounted, it's that simple. But when starting from the low-gun position, you often shoot over the top of the same easy target. The act of quickly lifting

The effect of
gun-mount impetus.

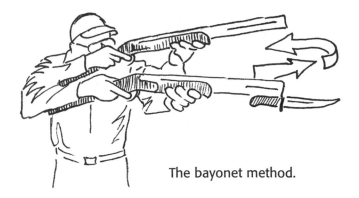

The bayonet method.

the gun imparts more upward impetus than you realize. That left-over momentum causes the point of impact of the shot to be higher than expected.

One solution that eliminates most of the angular momentum is to mount the gun with the same motion you'd use if you were trying to bayonet the bird in the rear end. Thrust the barrels forward, then pull the butt stock back into your shoulder. That way, when the gun is mounted, all the upward impetus is gone. Improved form predictably results in improved performance. The more extraneous impetus you can remove from your gun mount, the better you'll shoot. Guaranteed.

To a greater or lesser degree, unintentional momentum affects every shot, every swing, every move you make with any shotgun. Here's where dynamic balance becomes an important consideration. Back in chapter 4, a dynamically balanced shotgun was described as one with much of its weight located between the shooter's hands (referred to there as Mister Centerweight). A gun with that configuration comes up without a lot of extraneous impetus, and it's easy to control. Such a gun is more responsive because it builds up less impetus when put into motion.

WOODCOCK, TIMING, AND THE SECOND SHOT

A shooting acquaintance had brought his son with him to shoot five-stand. The teenager was intent on shooting at targets as soon as they cleared the trap. It appeared that he wanted to be known as the fastest gun in the East. It was impressive when he hit one, but he missed far more than he hit.

His dad saw me smiling at the boy's technique and leaned over from the adjoining shooting stand. "Talk to him, will you? When I try to tell him anything, it's just his old man blabbering. See if you can get through to him."

I had brought one of the setters with me that day. Later, when the boy came around to pet the dog, I sat with him on the tailgate of my truck, away from the other shooters. We talked about dogs and bird hunting, and after a while, I obliquely approached the boy's shooting method.

"It sure is fun to get those targets quick, isn't it?" I asked.

"That's what I like best," he answered.

"I can see that. I know a few other guys who like to shoot 'em quick. It's pretty cool when it happens right. I used to be Mr. Quick-shot myself, but then I decided that I'd rather be known as the guy who breaks 'em all."

The boy's expression froze.

"I'll take you out woodcock hunting with me in the fall," I offered. "You'll see what I mean. There'll be some chances that need to be taken quick—birds that are going to disappear behind some evergreens, or the first half of a pair in the thick stuff. But the great lesson that woodcock will teach you is that when you've got time, take time. Sometimes they fly like a knuckleball, but if you can watch 'em for a while, you can figure 'em out.

"The same is true with this target game, " I continued. "Some shots need to be taken quickly before they can turn into something much more difficult, but most of the time, you can do better if you follow the flight for just a moment like you would with a woodcock. I'm not saying you should ride the bird—that's a mistake of a different kind. But to hit a target you need to find the line, and you won't find it unless you look for it. And looking takes a moment or two. Shooting without knowing the line is like shooting without looking—it's just guessing."

I don't know if I got through to him. I haven't seen him since that day, but my invitation to take him hunting still stands. So does the great woodcock lesson: when you've got time, take time.

Woodcock shooting is all a matter of timing. Often they appear to be dodging on purpose as they dip and swerve, flitting their way through the treetops. When a hunter tries to track a woodcock's flight with the gun mounted, the comparison to a ballplayer trying to hit a knuckleball is never more apropos. Here's another example of the need for the previously mentioned compact swing. When it's done correctly, an uninitiated observer might think that the gun's firing mechanism is located in the butt plate. Follow the bird with the gun at ready, then, when the time is right, mount and shoot quickly. That's good advice for all shotgun shooting, but it's especially applicable to the unpredictable dips and dives of a woodcock in flight.

At other times, when a space in the leafy canopy offers an open escape route, woodcock fly deliberately toward that opening, and their line of flight becomes obvious and predictable. Such variations teach hunters to take time when they've got time but to be quick when the shot demands it. Woodcock shooting in the coverts of the Northeast is a mix of both sorts of shots, sometimes within moments of each other.

Woodcock can be deceptive. They pretend to be fast, but in reality, they are the slowest of all gamebirds. They would be easy to hit if they were found out on the grasslands, where a gunner might be able to follow the bird's line of flight. But instead, they inhabit scrubby, second-growth aspen stands and alder runs and places where they're often out of sight long before they're out of gun range.

Grouse and woodcock are often found in the same coverts. Most woodcock are hit by shooting right at them—no lead required. Of course, most grouse are missed for the same reason. The late Frank Woolner once said that if grouse are the high-performance fighter jets of the gamebird world, then woodcock are bi-wing stunt planes. Putting the two diametrically opposed birds in the same covert is one of those cosmic jokes that nature plays on us, although I don't recall laughing much when I've had a lot of empty shells in my game bag and no feathers to go along with them.

Each year, I manage to get two or three opportunities to take a double on woodcock. Certainly, those chances aren't as frequent as they are on doves or ducks or quail, but the advice on taking more than one target is the same for all: to succeed, you have to make two *complete* shots. That is, the first shot must consist of a beginning and an end that includes target acquisition, gun mount and swing, and follow-through; then the second shot must have all the same components. In baseball, most errors occur when an infielder begins his throw before he has fielded the ball. Similarly, failure on double opportunities is usually the result of beginning the second shot before the first is completed.

Double chances are exciting, and that excitement can cause anyone to rush, from seasoned veterans to the greenest rookies. However, the methodical way of shooting a double must include a momentary unshouldering of the gun and a start-from-scratch second shot. It's something that can be practiced on the skeet range, and that rehearsal will pay dividends on covey flushes and decoying mallards and, once in a while, in woodcock coverts.

When a follow-up shot is needed, even good shots often have trouble hitting with the second barrel. One theory is that they expect to hit the bird with the first shot and are genuinely surprised when it doesn't fall. Lesser shooters have doubts whenever they mount the gun, so they're prepared to pull the trigger as many times as necessary.

How can you practice second-barrel follow-up shooting? On the skeet field—when you're practicing and when it won't unnerve other shooters—use the second barrel to shoot the biggest piece of a target you broke with your first shot. That piece of broken target often has a different flight line and speed, so it requires a complete refocusing of your attention. Shooting a round of skeet in this manner can take an extra 10 or 15 shells, but it's a good drill that will pay dividends in the field. It's also a cure for the bad habit of coming out of the gun (discussed later in this chapter). And it's lots of fun.

DOVES AND WATERFOWL, THE COMPACT SWING, AND THE RAINBOW EFFECT

Pass shooting at ducks on their way to somewhere else can be a real test of shotgunning ability. Mallards in deliberate flight cruise along at the national speed limit, and geese fly faster than that. I've read that the canvasback is the fastest of all, but I've also read the same claim for the red-breasted merganser. (Maybe so, but if we could arrange a duck race, I'd put my money on the oldsquaw duck.) Estimating ranges and leads can be a challenge when there's nothing to measure against but the overcast sky. My father once assessed the right lead this way: "double whatever you think it is, then give it a little more for good measure."

The only similarities between doves and waterfowl are the types of shots a shotgunner might have at them. Both are shot as they pass, and both are sometimes taken over decoys. Flighting doves as they pass over a field can be as challenging as pass shooting at ducks, with similar long and fast shots. Doves have a darting way of flying, particularly once they realize they're being shot at. By one estimate, more ammunition is spent on doves than on all other gamebirds put together.

Unless there's a huge wind blowing, finding the right line of a passing duck or dove isn't usually a problem. The most common cause for missing such pass shots is not maintaining the swing speed. As in the extreme crossing shots at skeet, when you get as far in front as these targets require, you sometimes chicken out and slow the muzzle for a peek back at the target. To be consistently successful, you must believe in your lead and trust your swing.

Doves are relatively easy to kill. They're not tough birds, and they often fall to light loads. But there is an awfully small naked bird underneath those gray feathers, and ranges at passing doves are seldom predictable. Do what you must to ensure a sufficient pattern density to make consistent kills. My dove-hunting friends use light field loads of number 8 shot but elect to use fairly tight chokes—skeet-two or modified or even tighter.

The one thing that complicates both dove and waterfowl hunting is that it is often done while sitting down. That's a welcome situation between shots—it's nice to be comfortable—but it always works against the shooter when the time comes to actually do some trigger pulling. Your natural quadrant is severely limited when you're on your duff because of the inability to pivot with your hips. Standing is better, and better yet is a situation that provides legroom to make the one-step. That consideration ought to be at the top of the list whenever a shooting blind is constructed, but it rarely is.

The same birds when taken over decoys are an entirely different game. The shots are rarely difficult, but unlike other shotgunning endeavors, the targets are slowing rather than accelerating and dropping rather than rising. For a gunner used to aiming somewhere in front of the bird's beak, having to size up a lead below the bird's feet can take some practice.

Waterfowl may be the toughest gamebirds to kill outright, and that's especially true of diving ducks on big water. They're compact and heavily feathered, and they dump into the decoys on back-slanting wings rather than the gliding descent-under-power of puddle ducks and geese. It's a rare diver that's brought in with a broken wing. If you don't kill them outright, you've got to contend with their considerable talent as submarines. Ducks should be held to the same standard as all other gamebirds—dead on arrival is the only acceptable result, and the measure of effectiveness in waterfowling is consistency. To be killed reliably, ducks need to be hit with a big load of big shot from a big gun. Choke as tightly as you must, and use a load that's heavy enough to do the job.

Complicating things further is that ducks, geese, and doves are social birds and often decoy as a flock. Among the swirling multitude, there's usually one obvious bird—one decoyer that seems to be wearing a sign that says "shoot me." Unfortunately, both you and your shooting partner see it and end up shooting the same bird.

Then there's the perception that, at 200 yards, geese look large enough to hit with a thrown rock. At 60 yards, you can often see incoming geese looking right at you, and when they're actually in shotgun range, geese can seem frighteningly huge. Gunners miss when they assume that they only have to shoot somewhere in the vicinity to kill something that big. When killed cleanly, geese often hit the ground forward of the entire decoy spread—evidence that they might slow down but never lose their considerable forward motion, and proof that it's always a mistake to shoot right at them.

Sometimes, while the birds are coming in, you have a bit of time to mentally rehearse what you need to do. But that rehearsal time is both the blessing and bane of this type of shooting. Hunters often fall victim to the mistake of "riding the bird," with the resultant "rainbowing" of their swing. Shotgunning, of course, requires the gun to be moved in a straight line. Unfortunately, all human motions are the result of a pivoting action and trace a rainbowlike arc. Baseball players and golfers use the natural curve of the swinging motion to their advantage. Shotgunners seem to deny it exists—we continue to attempt to track straight-line targets with a naturally curving motion.

Not you? With an unloaded gun, try to swing the muzzle along the seam where the wall meets the ceiling. You'll find that you can't follow the straight line—at least not for very long. As you pivot, you inadvertently pull off the target's line. The longer the swing, the more pronounced the rainbow effect. Good shooting form—that is, keeping the right elbow up—can mitigate the problem. Nevertheless, all attempts at a long, flat-line swing without rainbowing result in the tangled knot becoming untied. The lesson of this exercise is that it's *always* a mistake to ride the bird. One of my two objections to skeet is that it encourages—even rewards—a shooter for the bad practice of riding the target. (The other is that it promotes the bad habit of mounting the gun before the target is acquired.)

A short, compact swing is the cure for rainbowing. It's the correct way to shoot ducks maneuvering into decoys, approaching doves, and every other target as well. Track the target with the gun down as you're waiting for the shot to develop. Then, as the sweet spot in time arrives, mount the gun with a swinging motion and shoot as soon as the butt hits your shoulder—there should be no hesitation. The line of the bird is determined before you mount the gun, and the swing-through is built into a proper gun mount. It doesn't come naturally without some practice, but it's the most consistent way to get results. Otherwise, the rainbow will get you.

One target-shooting mistake that can be carried over into field shooting is the practice of "coming out of the gun." Shooters are

Rainbowing the gun.

in such a hurry to get the gun off the shoulder that they dismount before the shot is complete, resulting in an abbreviated swing and follow-through. The practice can often be traced to some part of the gun mount that is uncomfortable: the shooter has a sore back that feels better when standing upright, or the shooter is being kicked by the gun's recoil and wants to get the gun away from his face as soon as possible (a real possibility with the heavy loads used in water-fowling or with the quantity of shots fired at doves). But just as often, coming out of the gun is the result of someone "styling" and trying to be cool. Done voluntarily, it's a practice that makes no more sense than a cowboy twirling his six-shooter on his finger.

Whatever the reason, coming out of the gun amounts to a pre-mature untying of the tangled knot. Once it becomes a habit, the anticipation of coming out begins to affect proper lead and timing, and it makes follow-up shots all but impossible. When your body is getting ready to come out of the gun, you're unconsciously slowing the swing. Like other bad habits, you might be unaware of it. The cure for this one is a dose of the universal shotgunning antidote: the exaggerated follow-through, as discussed in chapter 2.

Since we've touched on the subject of recoil problems, this might be a good place to address recovery time. Shooting a shotgun involves a brief shock that you must recover from before a second shot can be made. The shock, of course, is the gun's recoil, and recovery time varies with the weight of the gun, how well it fits you, and the strength of the load being used. It can be mild to severe, but there's no escaping it—the gun is going to kick you a bit.

Target shooters are much more familiar with recovery times than bird hunters are, because they routinely take targets as pairs. A logical strategy employed in the target games is to use a lighter load in the first barrel to minimize recovery time. Hunters might argue that an even better strategy is to make a good first shot and thus make the second shot unnecessary, and I'd be the first to agree with that sentiment. For those who remain unconvinced by arguments against the need for high-velocity and magnum loads, a good compromise might be to save such loads for the second shot and use something lighter on the first.

PHEASANTS AND TARGET ANGULARITY

Hunters know that bird dogs come in two subsets: flushing dogs and pointing dogs. The one big difference—in this book, at least—is the sort of shot you might expect when hunting behind each. Pointing dogs can and do point pheasants. Sometimes the bird is right where the dog says it is, and the hunter gets the classic steep-rising shot depicted in every pheasant-hunting scene ever painted. That's what hunters hope for, anyway. But more often than not, Mr. Ringneck lives up to his reputation as a runner and doesn't stay pinned for long. Often, when hunters walk in expecting an underfoot flush, they find that the bird has slipped away, leaving them with the sort of 40-yard shot you might see at the trap range—or something a lot farther. If you're operating with your own effective slot in mind, such shots are tough to justify.

High-one as a pheasant shot.

Pheasants over a flushing dog are a different story. When things work out as they're supposed to, the hunter's shots become a matter of timing the rooster's two-part rise. The birds use their powerful legs to spring into the air and climb 20 feet straight up. Then, when their upward momentum runs out, they adjust their posture to begin level flight. Timing is about anticipating the pause or waiting until the bird begins level flight, which resembles a high-one or high-two target. In that situation, leading the bird means shooting under it.

The two-part flush applies only to rooster pheasants. Hens (in places where they are legal game) are more challenging targets and seem to hold better for pointing dogs than do cocks. They come off the ground at close to top speed and slant away immediately. From my limited experience with prairie chickens and sharptails over pointing dogs, I can say that hen pheasants offer similar shots. Low seven (and its various permutations) is the shot you have to master. If anything, crank more altitude into the trap so that you see shots that rise more steeply. As with all rising shots, the most common error involves lifting your head as soon as you can't see the target anymore.

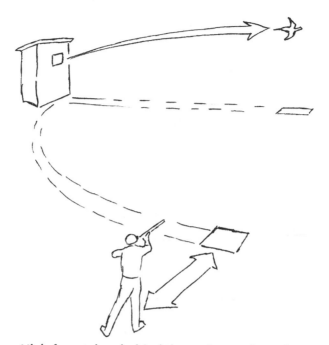

High-four, taken behind the pad, as a dove shot.

Pheasant shooters occasionally have shots at crossing birds and would do well to understand the extreme leads involved at station four. You can replicate long shots by backing up off the station a few paces, if your skeet club permits that sort of thing.

With any live bird, but particularly with one as large as a pheasant, some consideration must be given to angularity. Crossing birds present the largest silhouettes and are usually struck with a maximum number of pellets and thus with a maximum shock effect. After that, angularity comes into play. The effectiveness of any shotgun hit is subject to additive and subtractive angles. A bird flying away from the shooter takes energy away from the shock effect, and one flying toward the shooter adds its momentum to the collision, amplifying the effect.

At first, the business of angles seems like nitpicking. A bird traveling 30 miles per hour is being overtaken by a shot swarm going 500 miles per hour, so the influence of the flight angle seems like a minor point. But then consider that the effect of shock is mass *times* velocity. An incoming bird adds its mass to the shock-effect multiplier, and one going away subtracts its mass from the equation. Engineers like to prove such things with numbers, but if you've hunted for a while, you don't need numbers to tell you that incomers are usually dead before they hit the ground, and going-away birds are the toughest to kill cleanly, even at moderate range.

Beneath every gamebird's layer of feathers is a much smaller target, but the illusion of size is never more pronounced than with very small birds. If you could see a naked dove or quail fly by, you wouldn't need much convincing to ditch the coarse shot. Such tiny targets become smaller yet when the bird is flying straight away from you. Then, all you have to shoot at is the bird's rear end and its wings. If you can break a wing bone, the bird comes down; it's rarely dead, but at least it's on the ground. But even when you center such a going-away shot, you often hit only the legs and belly. That won't bring the bird down, because all the critical parts are at the other end of the bird. You might break a leg or put a couple of ultimately fatal pellets into the bird's gut, but unless you break a wing, the bird will keep flying, often like an unguided missile. A gut-hit bird is often dead where it ends up, but finding it isn't easy.

What can you do? Choke is the answer to this problem. Choke tight enough to provide sufficient pattern density and sufficient shock effect to overcome the subtractive effect of the bird's momentum. Let the easier shots fall where they may, but you need to know that you've got sufficient firepower to kill cleanly the toughest shot you expect to take—in this case, the 35-yard flat straightaway.

Knowing the right way to handle a difficult shooting situation and actually doing it can be entirely different things. We all make mistakes, and we will continue to make them in the future, despite our best intentions to the contrary. When that happens, it's helpful to know what we did wrong and what we can do to correct the problem.

Shots at wild birds are never routine, and because each one is different, we can never really "get in a groove." We all miss sometimes, but experience tends to stick to those who pay it the compliment of attention. Each time we shoot and miss, there's a lesson to be learned. Don't pass up the chance.

9

Clay Target Games and Self-Instruction

In his day, Uncle Ralph, pheasant hunter extraordinaire, was referred to by other men as a "good shot," and he might well have been. But then again, he might have been just a "good pheasant shot." There's a difference.

Pheasant shooting, of course, involves the sort of shots you usually get at pheasants. To be good at it, you need to master only two basic presentations: the station seven get-away shot and the steep climber. Each has several permutations, but pheasants are hardly aerial acrobats, and once in flight, they maintain predictable flight lines and steady speeds. There are occasional nonroutine opportunities, but pheasant shooting generally doesn't involve incomers, dropping shots, deceleration shots, multiple chances, or anything with a compound curve. Pheasant hunting is done in the open, so overhead shots and below-eye-level chances are mostly unknown, and too-close shots can be waited out.

I point this out not to demean pheasant shooting but to make the observation that the legendary Uncle Ralph might have been a specialist rather than a general practitioner. I have a nephew who is a marvelous waterfowl shot, but he doesn't do too well when I take him grouse and woodcock hunting. Like Uncle Ralph, he's very good at the variations of the several shots he routinely encounters but has little proficiency outside his area of expertise.

119

Every gamebird has its standard menu of presentations, and after a while, the standard shots become fairly routine. Quail shooting is fast and nerve-racking, but it presents just two basic scenarios; the same can be said for decoying ducks. Pass shooting is challenging, but the menu of shots is fairly predictable. Woodcock can be tricky, but once you get the hang of the timing, the shots are almost repetitious. Goose shooting is spectacular but rarely challenging. It might be argued that grouse shooting offers a shotgunner a full menu, but none of the distances are even medium-range shooting—it's all close or not at all. The best grouse shooters I know don't do well at anything longer than skeet-range distances.

For most of us, being as good as Uncle Ralph would be good enough. But then we go to a sporting clays course and realize how many things can be done with a shotgun. The game of sporting clays dares you to put into practice everything you know about shotgun shooting, and maybe a few things you haven't learned yet. The shots cover the full menu of possibilities—near and far, high and low, angles and straightaways, steep climbers and falling targets, and long shots launched from a tower. Some opportunities have to be allowed to develop, while others must be taken quickly. There are mini-targets that seem no bigger than a bumblebee as they pass, bouncing below-eye-level rabbit targets, and razor-thin battues that skim along with the aerodynamic properties of a flat rock.

When setting up sporting clays courses, clever managers attempt to challenge the shooter's ability to properly control the shotgun's impetus. They might arrange the targets' flight paths so that the gun has to swing in one direction for the first shot, then move along a line in the opposite direction to take the second target. Or, equally challenging, they might arrange targets with the second following the first at a pace that causes the gunner to successively move the muzzles back and forth. Shooting instructors speak of the Z move or the L move to describe these herky-jerky swings. Move too quickly, and you won't be accurate; move too slowly, and the target is out of range. The best targets test your gun-handling skills, not just your marksmanship.

If you want to become a good shot, you must become intimate with clay targets. Skeet is where you learn the fundamentals of marksmanship. Clays is where you figure out how to apply those fundamentals to nonroutine situations. When shooting, you must constantly make decisions, and there is a series of questions to be asked and answered at every new station. If you pursue sporting clays, you'll become aware of all that and more.

Competition demands standardization, but so far, sporting clays has resisted uniformity. Like golf, every course is similar yet different. A refreshing aspect of the game is that even the best shooters miss—not as often as you and I, of course. But in sporting clays, missing a few doesn't immediately brand you a novice, as it might at the competitive levels of skeet or trap. Winning scores at sporting clays tournaments are in the 80s or 90s—nobody goes 100 straight.

The game of five-stand is an attempt to bring the challenges of sporting clays to a skeet-type setup. Five shooting stands are lined up, and a menu of targets is presented, with a single and two pairs shot from each box. To be officially sanctioned, a five-stand setup must have certain target presentations (a rabbit target, a springing teal, a going-away off a tower, an incomer, a left-to-right, and a right-to-left), but the combinations can be as varied as the target-setter wishes, and five-stand can be every bit as challenging as any sporting clays course. Like clays, decisions need to be made on every station, and you will be challenged to use all your skills with a shotgun—only without all the walking.

When William Harnden Foster and his buddies invented the game of skeet, they intended it as practice for grouse shooting. As a grouse hunter, I have shot skeet to stay in practice all my adult life, but my shooting moved to the next level 15 years ago when I took up the innovative game known as modern skeet. The modern game takes place on a standard skeet field, but the machines that fling the targets are mounted on vertically oscillating platforms. The targets are thrown in the same direction as in traditional skeet, but the angle of flight is unpredictable: the shooter doesn't know whether it will be a low grass-skimmer, a steep rising shot, or something in between. It varies with the constantly changing angle of the trap.

In chapter 8, I wrote of the brain's ability to recognize the one place on the target's flight line that will be the point of interception—the sweet spot in time. The allure of modern skeet is that you don't know where the sweet spot is going to occur; some shots develop leisurely, while others require a hurry-up reaction. As in bird hunting, the game rewards the gunner who cultivates the skill of rapidly acquiring the target and interpreting the line to find the sweet spot. As such, premounting the gun actually works *against* you. Dyed-in-the-wool skeeters hate the unpredictable aspect of the modern game, but it's what Foster wished skeet could be: find the target, identify the line, make the shot.

It is widely believed that anything and everything you can do with your shotgun will make you a better shot. Trap-shooting comes close to being the exception. Trap involves just one very long shot and its angled variations. It might be considered practice for shooting pheasants or some other bird that runs and flushes at long range, but the distance involved is on the cusp of being too far, or perhaps a little beyond. In the field, bird hunters who are aware of their slots and the effective range of their shotguns routinely pass up the sort of shot seen on the trap range. Back in the good old days, trap involved boxed pigeons (that is, actual live birds with feathers) that were released and shot at from a distance similar to modern-day trap. The clay target form of trap started as practice for the real thing.

In its evolution, the game of trap spawned the trap gun, which is a sport-specific tool designed for one job only: to break trap targets. It is heavy by design, to absorb the recoil of an afternoon's shooting of a hundred rounds or more, and it is tightly choked to be effective at trap's extreme ranges. Since gun movement is minimal (the gun is mounted before the target is called for), the design sacrifices balance and nimbleness in favor of a long, weight-forward sighting plane. But what really makes the trap gun unsuited to anything else is that it is made to shoot high. By design, the point of impact is above the sighting plane—something that would be a disastrous problem in any other gun. Trap shooters want such a contrivance to be able to float the target above the gun's rib and not lose sight of it until it breaks. Thus, the trap gun has a built-in compensation for the predictable amount of rise seen in trap targets. Nearly every shotgun that is currently manufactured is available in just such a high-shooting "trap model." Universally, they are long-barreled, high-stocked, heavier versions of the standard.

Of course, you don't need a trap gun to shoot trap. But with a standard shotgun—one that hits where it's pointed—such rising targets would have to be blotted out as you pulled the trigger and lifted the gun. Because you naturally want to see the target break, you would start peeking, which equates to missing. That's why dedicated trap shooters want bona fide trap guns, and why their method of floating the rising target translates to a bad habit in all other forms of shotgunning.

There's a life lesson that I learned years ago, and I find myself retelling the story often. It applies to the recognition of mistakes. I was a young chief engineer on a seagoing tanker and was spending a week at a firefighting school on the campus of Texas A&M. The school went to great lengths to arrange simulations of shipboard fires, and although the situation was staged, the fire was very real, as were the heat, the noise, and the fear felt by us guys with the fire hoses.

In this particular instance, I led two hose teams out into a shallow pool on top of which was a floating layer of diesel oil that had been set ablaze. We were supposed to use high-velocity fog nozzles to push the fire back across the pool so that we could reach a structure, where a valve needed to be shut off to stop the "leak" of diesel oil into the pool. That was the plan. Unfortunately, the Texas wind shifted after we entered the pool, and our progress was stopped halfway across. We stood there up to our knees in oil—seven men in full firefighting gear—unable to do more than hold the wall of fire at bay. After a long 3-minute standoff, someone grabbed the ear hole of my helmet and shouted above the noise of the pair of 2½-inch hoses, "Are you putting out the fire, Mulak?" It was the instructor, dressed in gym shorts and a T-shirt. Usually he stayed on the sidelines, but in this case, he recognized a problem and thought it necessary to wade out into the diesel pool. I was dumbfounded. I could only shake my head.

"Then why the hell don't you try something different?" he shouted.

Good question. Why the hell *didn't* I try something different? Obviously, what I was doing wasn't working.

It isn't often that we're given a piece of wisdom that can guide us through the rest of our lives, but there it is: if what you're doing isn't working, try something different. If you put a good lead on a target and miss, for goodness' sake, don't do the same thing again. One of the definitions of insanity is to keep repeating an action with the expectation of a different result. Try something different. Miss again if you must, but at least miss for a different reason. Don't make the same mistake twice.

That seems obvious, but often you can't bring yourself to believe that the last shot—the one that felt so right when you pulled the trigger—didn't hit. Maybe there was something wrong with the pattern, you tell yourself. You call for another bird and do the same thing again and, of course, miss again. Finally, right around the time you realize what you're doing wrong, the guy with the score sheet says, "That's it. You're done. Get out of the box. Who's next?"

Whenever you shoot clay targets, don't lose sight of the idea that you're honing your skills. Don't be afraid to miss, as long as something can be learned from the miss. If your local skeet club has an installation for modern skeet, you can adjust the trap machines to throw just about any target you want. You might have to buy a case of shells and spend an entire weekend working on just one problem. Tell yourself that the ammunition is the cost of putting that particular problem behind you.

When trying to correct a specific problem on a specific shot, search for fundamental errors. For instance, if you always miss high two but hit everything else fairly regularly, your problem isn't that you don't know how much lead to give that particular target. Rather, there's something very basic that you're doing incorrectly—pulling the gun away from your face (untying the tangled knot) or, more likely, misinterpreting the line of the bird. There might be a disconnect between what you *think* you're doing and what is actually happening. In this age of ubiquitous video cameras, sometimes a simple 1-minute video clip taken while you're shooting can reveal something you didn't even realize you were doing wrong.

When it comes to shooting, don't be afraid to admit that you might need some help. Let's use the baseball analogy again. Most of us have played baseball. Some of us may have more natural ability than others, but there has never been a ballplayer who couldn't benefit from instruction. Each major league team's hitting coach draws a handsome salary for helping guys who already hit well enough to play in the major leagues. The message here is that no matter how good you are, you might be even better with the help of a shooting instructor. Good instructors are skilled in recognizing and correcting problems. The instructor doesn't even have to be a professional. I have several friends who are methodical enough about shooting fundamentals that I'm always willing to listen to their advice. Sometimes they point out things that I don't even realize I'm doing.

Whether you act as your own teacher or take lessons, you need to adopt the motto that there are no mistakes, only lessons. There is something to be learned from every missed shot. Be clever enough to realize that. Remember, too, that although someone can give you instructions, being able to carry them out requires practice. You'll get better only at those things you actually practice.

Some people are forever searching for a magic bullet, switching from number 8s to 8½s or some other minutia in the hope that it will improve their game. They seek to become good shots when they haven't yet mastered the basics of shooting well. They think that there's some trick to it and are always searching for a shortcut. There's a quote by Sir William Russell Flint, a famous British watercolorist, that applies here: "Amateurs are apt to believe that if only they knew the tricks they would be very good painters, but ten thousand tricks will never make an artist."

The same thing can be said about shotgunning. There are tricks and tips, but they don't amount to much if you can't find the line and keep the gun moving. If you can master those two fundamentals, you can accomplish what you set out to do. You can become a good shot.

INDEX